ECHO OF THE TOM TOMS

BY
MRS. FRANCES LEBRET

GENEALOGY

Indians were first here between 13AD and 1700

1730   Introduction of horses to the Pacific Northwest.

1782   First smallpox epidemic.

1790s LeBlanc and Le Gasse were the first white men to visit the Colville and Spokane Indians. They were French fur traders

1805   Lewis and Clark expedition.

Grey Cloud is the Uncle of Blue Bird.

Falling Leaf is the sister of Grey Cloud and the mother of three children, one of which is Blue Bird.

Chief Eagle Eye is the husband of Falling Leaf and friend to Grey Cloud.

1811   Jacob Stewart built a primitive cabin of driftwood where the Okanogan and Columbia River join. It was the first trading post in the interior.

1812   Astor established a trading post at the mouth of the Spokane River.

1828   Around 1828 Fred Perkins was born in New

York to Capt. Perkins and his wife.

1840s Uncle Samuel took over the shipping
business when his brother died. It was about
the same time that Red Wing was born in
the 1840s.

1840 First child of Falling Leaf and Eagle Eye is
born. They name her Owl Eyes.

Elkanah and Mary Walker, called Priest by
the Indians, came to the area at about the
same time Owl Eyes was born. Also,
Reverend Eels Cushing came. They built
Tshimakian Mission on Tshimakian Creek. It
emptied into the Spokane River. (founded in
1838 and closed 10 years later) It was located
near present Springdale, Washington.

1842-03 A second child was born to Eagle Eye and
Falling Leaf. They named her Blue Bird.

A third child, Red Wing, was born a few
years later.

1845 Fred Perkins went to sea with his Uncle
Samuel much to the chagrin of his mother.
The Perkins' family was reasonably wealthy
and Fred's mother wanted her son to be a
doctor.

1847 Measles epidemic in the Colville and
Spokane Indian tribes.

1848   The Tshimakian mission is discontinued.

1850   Samuel Perkins ship docked in San
       Francisco, California where Fred was
       shanghaied.

1851   Fred and other shipmates were dumped
       somewhere south of San Francisco off the
       California coast.

1852   Fred made it back to New York. He began
       training to become a doctor.

1855 or so - Fred got a commission from the U.S.
       Government to go West to McDonald Block
       House near Marcus, Washington.

1856   Fred Perkins saved Blue Bird from drowning
       in the Columbia River. She was about five.

1857   Measles epidemic.

1858   Battle at Steptoe Butte.

       Fred was helping to build the first
       steamboat (paddle) to navigate the Columbia
       River. It went as far north as the Arrow
       lakes in British Columbia.

       There was a Small Pox epidemic in the
       Spokane Indian Tribe.

       Old Kettle Falls

Fred founded a school in Marcus, Washington. It was the first in Stevens County.

1860　Blue Bird attended Fred's school. She may have been nine. Grey Cloud is at Marcus and is the caregiver to Blue Bird, her mother and her two sisters.

1861　Civil War.

1864　Fred asks Blue Bird to marry him in spite of the hostile resistance of Grey Cloud. Grey Cloud's family is made up of his two older sons, his sister Falling Leaf and her three children; Owl Eyes, Blue Bird and Red Wing.

That same year Fred and Blue Bird were married. She may have been as young as 13 and he as old as 28.

1868　Blue Bird escapes Grey Cloud and returns to Fred at Marcus, Washington.

1869　Christine is born to Fred and Blue Bird.

1870　Fred and his family move to Walker's Prairie on Chimokane Creek. It is the line between Spokane and Stevens County.

1877　Chief Joseph of the Nez Perce led the last organized fight against the white man and the U.S. Government. He was born in 1840 and died in 1904.

1879   Fred and his family were still at Walker's Prairie.

WYNECOOP FAMILY

1828   John Wynecoop was born.

1848   John Wynecoop lived with his family on a nice farm in Galesburg, Illinois. John got Gold Fever and left for California.

1851   John returned to his family in Illinois.

1856   Curtis was one of five children born to the Wynecoop family.

1858   The Battle of Steptoe Butte.

1860   John and Mandy Wynecoop joined the Western movement for California.

1860s Grey Cloud and his group were in the Midwest where John Wynecoop and his family were traveling on a wagon train. Eagle Eye was killed in a drunken brawl with his own people.

Amos Wells was in a second wagon train behind the Wynecoop wagons and was the only one to escape when Grey Cloud, the

Indian on the unusually beautiful black horse, and his group attacked the second wagon train.

The wagon train split and some went to Oregon and some went to California. The Wynecoops, John and Mandy and their five children went to California.

1865   Lizzy, one of the Wynecoop children, died, closely followed by her father, John.

1879   Curt is now 20 years old. He worked in Texas as a cowboy for a number of years and then returned to California and on to Oregon ending up in Sprague, Washington. He chased a herd of wandering cattle through Davenport and up the river to Walker's Prairie.

Grey Cloud is still alive and Christine, great niece of Grey Cloud, marries Curt Wynecoop.

1882   Blue Bird dies at about age 39.

1884   Fred Perkins dies at about the age of 56. He's still poor but happy with his life.

The daughter of Curt and Christine Perkins Wynecoop was Frances.

Frances Wynecoop married James Le Bret.

1910   James Le Bret and Francis Wynecoop Le

Bret had a daughter. They named her "Millie."

1939 "Millie" married Herb Lyons. Millie died in 1992 and Herb in 1997.

1940 Joe Lyons is born.

ECHOE OF THE TOM TOMS

TABLE OF CONTENTS

Chapter 1 – Introduction

The night was dark, for there was no moon. Stars were shining brightly, but their light was not strong enough to penetrate the thick darkness of dense forest, and the campfires scattered here and there amongst the Teepees gave the Indians all the light they needed.

Surrounded so completely by the friendly forest, this little Indian village was far from the prying eyes of white people, and that was just the way the Indians liked it. Here a scene was being enacted, which, had anyone seen and understood, would have struck terror to the strongest of hearts.

An Indian war dance was being held with all the hideousness and abandonment of the most savage of tribes with an utter disregard to civilization in any form. It was being conducted in a strictly Indian fashion and according to their own beliefs, dating back to the beginning of time for them.

The dance was as interesting to behold as it was fearful for there were many warriors, although on this particular night they were not preparing for war. However, the thought of war was always present in these troublous days and a dance held just for the sake of pleasure differed very little from that of the real war dance. They were planning a buffalo hunt the next day and who knows what they might run into, besides buffalo.

The men were all decked out in feathers and greasy

paint of many colors and with tinkling ornaments strung and tied around their necks. They wore beautifully decorated moccasins and a breach cloth, which constituted their costumes for this or any other occasion.

Nearby sat some of the older men around a large drum, or tom-tom. They were loudly beating the tom-tom with wooden drumsticks and, to this regular, deep-toned, surprisingly perfect rhythm, the hilarious dancers kept time with their swiftly moving feet.

The Tom-tom was made of hard dry buffalo skin, tanned to a shiny finish and stretched over the end of a hollow log or over the top of a hollow stump. It made a deep echoing sound that reverberated through the woods and over the prairies for many miles, chilling the hearts of any unfortunate white people who might be within hearing distance.

As the braves danced they leaped and swayed, sometimes bent almost double, turning this way and the other, with heads held high, with the bright firelight shining on their faces painted in many colors in striped and frightfully grotesque designs, laughing and singing in the joy and freedom that only children and people who are free from all bondage can feel.

Grey Cloud, who stood silently in the shadows refusing to join with his friends or even to let them know he was there, was not being fooled by anyone. Let them have their fun if they felt that way. It was a good pastime and time meant nothing to them! He was glad his people were still able to enjoy themselves. As for him, time meant a lot, if he could only use it for the one purpose that lay so desperately close to his heart, to drive the white people out and bring back the peace and freedom they had once known.

As he stood watching the lively dancers, the women entered into the sport. They were more quiet and their dancing performances more simple. Their long dresses were made of buckskin and trimmed with rows of fringe, also of buckskin, some around the shoulders and some on the skirts. These costumes were lavishly trimmed with beads made of porcupine quills in different colors. The costumes were very effective with the long black braids hanging down their backs or over each shoulder, while across the brow of some were head bands trimmed to match the dresses.

This dance was very quiet, for the women stood side-by-side all facing the same direction, sometimes in a circle, while they sang their Indian songs in quiet but sweet tones.

While singing they kept perfect time with their feet, which were encased in beautiful moccasins. They moved inch by inch, all in one direction, some of them smiling and others taking it all very seriously. Although their dance was not nearly so exciting nor as fantastic as that of the men, it was all for the same purpose.

Regardless of what tonight or tomorrow might hold for them, it was a war dance, reminding them that many more lives might be added to the long list of war dead before many more days had gone by, including some of their own loved ones.

These were some of the thoughts that were passing through the mind of Grey Cloud as he stood watching the dancers. He looked to see if there was any of the white man's fire water fire in evidence and when he saw that all was as it should be, he turned and went back to his teepee, where he stretched out on a buffalo hide. For a while he lay thinking, then he dropped off to sleep. When he awoke, it was still dark, although the sky was beginning to show the light of a beautiful morning. Silently he arose and went out to look around. The dance had come to an end and the weary merrymakers were all asleep in their tepees. Stealthily he crept out and went out of the sleeping village in the direction of his ponies.

He soon located one and, in a twinkling was on his back and, with a rawhide rope for a bridle, he was off. He was restless and sad for he was thinking of the days when he and his brothers had wept when they called on their gods for help, but either the gods could not hear them or were too busy to help them and they were becoming more discouraged and hopeless every day. As he rode slowly along he was deep in thought and his thoughts were far from being pleasant.

"White men! White men! Strange men with skins of

white but hearts as black as night!" mused the young Indian savagely, as he gazed, in the early dawn, over the wide spreading prairies which lay smoothly before him, almost like a bright green carpet dotted here and there with beautiful wild flowers.

His prairies! His land! His home!!! The home of his ancestors and all his loved ones. How happy they had been, and now - these rolling prairies, the distant mountains, and nearby hills and valleys, the distant forests they all loved so well and on which they depended so much for many of the necessities of life, were being invaded more and more by the white people, and they were doing it in the name of civilization, a word that he could not comprehend, for the little good that it contained so far overshadowed by the bad it held that he wanted none of it. The enemy came in swarms and try as they might they found that there was no halting them, for their primitive methods of war were powerless against the white man's thunder weapon, as onward the white man came, slowly but surely winning the west. In deep despair the young Indian bowed his head. He made a striking figure as he stood beside his spotted Pony. The feathers on his head were brightly colored and his strong body was decorated with figures and stripes of many colors. Outwardly he was calm and collected, and except for his eyes, which were sharp and piercing, there was no signs of any inward struggles. But his heart was like a pent-up volcano, a fever of hate and defeat. He covered his face with his hands and his powerful shoulders shook with his great grief. Then he turned blindly to his pony, standing quietly by, and springing lightly upon his back, he turned and rode swiftly toward the village, the place which was still home to him and where still dwelt the people who were dearer than life to him.

How long will they be allowed to live there was something that only time could tell. His sure-footed pony never slacked his pace as he galloped swiftly over the grass covered ground and it was only a short time until the village came in sight. As Grey Cloud drew near he was not surprised to find that the others were up and some had already caught their ponies and were preparing for the buffalo hunt. It did not take long to catch another pony, and after he disposed of the breakfast that his generous mother had prepared for him he was ready to go. His pony was coal black and Grey Cloud was very proud of him, but the thought of his ponies always sent a stab of pain through his heart for only a few months ago he had owned a fine herd and he had been very proud of it, until one day in a battle with the white man they had stolen, killed or burned nearly all of them including some of his most prized animals, and for this he was still very bitter and sullen. But buffalo hunting, so very full of excitement and thrills, gave him plenty to think about besides what the white men had done to him, although he never forgot that there might be some of those very people lurking along the way, watching for a chance to get some meat for themselves, meat that he did not think they had any right to, since they had no respect for what belonged to the Indians.

He knew that the white people would not merely be
hunting with bows and arrows as he did but would
have something much more fearful and destructive,
their terrible thunder weapons. Grey Cloud often
wished that he could own such a weapon and his
smoldering eyes would glisten as he thought of all
the things he could accomplish with one.

He knew of certain Indians who had been given
guns by white men but he didn't trust such Indians
and he felt that white men who helped the Indians
kill other white people, men, women and children,
were lower than the rattlesnake for they were
treacherous to the Indians and white people alike.
He knew that he would never be guilty of accepting
a gun from a white man but if he could steal one
from any white man he would gladly do so.

It was a perfect day for riding over the sloping hills,
green with the rich grass of early summer which
was dotted here and there with beautiful flowers of
the season. Along the gullies where the bushes
grew, thick and heavy, were lovely wild roses and
other blooming bushes in which numerous birds
twittered and sang. Wending its cheery way
through this restful setting rippled a lively
mountain stream of clear cold water and hiding
from view the swiftly darting spotted trout.

 Grey Cloud was thirsty so he dismounted and
leaving his pony free to get his fill with water and a
mouthful or two of green grass, he knelt down and
leisurely drank until he was satisfied; then, as the

pony shook himself, Grey Cloud stood up and raised his long arms towards the sky, took a good long stretch, then, grasping his pony by the mane, he lightly sprang onto his satiny back and proceeded to catch up with the others.

Finally, he caught sight of a Buffalo herd and, to Grey Cloud it was a beautiful sight. But the instant the Indian saw it the herd chase was on and with one movement the herd was stampeding across the prairie in an effort, however futile, to escape the flying arrows. Grey Cloud was a real hunter and was out to get meat for himself and others of the family but today the sight of so many animals rushing pell mell to escape troubled him a little and almost caused him to lose interest in the hunt. But by night he had bagged one huge buffalo and had assisted his friends in getting theirs. This turned out to be their lucky day for when they all got together after the chase they found that they had enough meat to last them for many days and there would be many more robes to keep them and their families warm. It had been a very lucky day in another way, too, for not a single white man had been seen to mar their pleasure, although Grey Cloud would far rather have been chasing white men than buffalo. He knew that the way he and his friends hunted the buffalo was the proper way for they only killed what they would use. The rest of the herd would live to serve them indefinitely. This was much better than running the whole herd over a high cliff as many of the white men did, crippling and wounding practically all of it just to get a few choice cuts of meat, slaughtering the rest for hides.

Just thinking of these things made Grey Cloud very angry and, while he gloated over the results of their big day's work, he growled savagely as he searched the distant horizon. But since there was no one in sight, he settled down to the work at hand, getting the meat and hides ready to carry home. As Grey Cloud looked at all the work spread out before him he grunted discontentedly. It was all very well for the Indian men to chase and kill the buffalo, that was their job. But other tribes that he knew of made their wives follow them, keeping a safe distance, of course, with their camping outfits, all prepared to take over the finishing up of the job. "Why couldn't his tribe do the same thing?" Of course, he had never heard the saying, "Man's work is from sun to sun but woman's work is never done" but if he had he probably would have said "That is as it should be;" for if there was anything he hated to do, it was what he considered as "woman's work."

But right now, there was nothing that he could do about it, so he grumbled and, not having any sleeves to roll up, he took hold of a huge buffalo and went to work with a will, doing just what he had to do and no more. The rest was definitely "woman's work" and they would take over from wherever he left off. What happened to the meat from then on until it was ready to eat was none of his business.

Meanwhile, back in the little Indian village to which the weary hunters were now returning, time had not been standing still for, to the women, it had been a busy day. The village itself was composed of many teepees, each one surrounded by a clean swept yard, where the black dirt was well packed by the treading of many feet. The teepees were made of buffalo hides, most of them tanned, some with a hard, smooth finish and others with a rather rough surface. Some were more plain white or a dull tan color and others were painted in a wild array of beautiful designs being very decorative against the background of the piney woods and all nature in its natural state, un-tampered by any so-called improvements.

Inside most of the teepees sat one or more old people who were quite content to sit and visit while some of them sewed as they talked and others just sat and smoked their long-stemmed pipes filled with dried kinnikinick leaves.

Standing some distance apart from the regular village was a very small teepee, also made of buffalo hides. In the center of it burned a warm fire made of dry sticks and other bits of fuel gathered from the woods nearby. The smoke did not interfere for it floated straight up to a hole at the top of the teepee where the poles met and were tied just as were the larger homes.

Beside the fire was a small basket made from the bark of a cottonwood or birch tree. Inside the basket was a soft downy substance which felt like the silk of the very finest, only finer. It had been gathered from the marsh not far from the village and was taken from the cat tails or tulles which grew so plentifully up there.

A young woman whose name was Falling Leaf lay
quietly on some robes against the wall while
several women sat around laughing and talking as
they waited patiently. No one was in a hurry. There
was no place to go and life was sweet, especially the
life of the young. But as they waited they kept their
fingers busy as well as their tongues for there was
always a lot of sewing to do. There was very little
time to waste for there were many feet of all sizes
to make moccasins for and every spare moment was
utilized in this way.

One of the things that had to be done after the men
had departed on their hunting trip was to get wood.
So, a group of women with raw hide ropes had gone
to the woods to get their supply for the day. This
they gathered up in piles and carried on their
backs. " Hard work?" but they didn't mind in the
least. They always took their time for time seldom
meant much to them. If they were lucky enough to
find a dry tree which had been blown over by the
wind they were happy indeed for this meant plenty
of wood for all. Otherwise they gathered what
limbs, roots or bark were available for they had no
way of cutting the trees down.

In the teepees, if it was cool, other women set
sewing: some making gloves or moccasins, others
making suits for the men or dresses for themselves;
all out of buckskin. Buckskin was made from deer
hides. Here and there were other women, old and
young, who were very busy on another important

job: that of tanning the hides into buckskin.

No matter how busy the women were, there was one thing that must not be forgotten nor neglected. When the men got home they would be tired and hungry, so they must have something ready for them to eat. With this thought in mind they carried on their work while planning and preparing their separate meals for the evening, watching the meat, which was already cooking, and superintending the grinding of roots and berries, which often fell to the younger people who were too young to do the more difficult jobs or to others who were too old to do much work of any sort.

In the meantime, back in the little teepee women laughed and joked with Falling Leaf, the sister of Grey Cloud. It had been just a year since her young man had brought a fine deer and laid it on her door mat, by way of confessing to her that she was the only girl in the world for him. His name was Eagle Eye and he was a very able young man, and also very handsome.

So, she had blushingly consented at the council meeting that followed a few weeks later. This made her his wife, according to the laws of the tribe, and was more binding than many of the more civilized marriage ceremonies, for it meant that all the big chiefs of the tribe were gathered there to unite two of their worthy young people in a marriage that knew no divorce, come good or bad, sickness or health, only death should ever draw her away from his side. If for any reason whatsoever, he should stray away from her hearth and home, she was to take the blame for not being able to hold her husband, and she would receive no sympathy from the tribe. Rather one-sided perhaps, but such was the law, although it did not frighten Falling Leaf, for well she knew that even though the brave may be master in his own right, the wife was mistress and would find more deer on her door mat as the years rolled by.

Eagle Eye was out with the hunters but that was just the way it should be for his wife was in good hands. If in secret he worried a little about her, he dared not let it be known, for birth was supposed to be a worry that concerned only the women.

But that evening when the hunters returned, weary and heavy laden with meat and buffalo hides, they found everybody smiling and happy. In the little teepee Falling Leaf smiled weakly as she gazed lovingly at the little bundle in the bark basket for cuddled down in the soft silky lining was a darling baby girl.

Only the young woman's mother remained with her now, for the others had all gone back to their teepees to prepare supper for their families. Falling Leaf did not need them anymore.

The meals cooked in the various homes were somewhat alike. It was good healthy, body building food as was proved by the stalwart young men bringing home the meat.

The fact that there were so many Indians at that
time was proof that the way they lived was a
healthy one and that the food they ate was good for
them. There was not a great variety to choose from
but they were not a bit choosy. Although on a night
such as this, with fresh meat in every home, they
would naturally all want fresh meat. All dried meat
or salmon would be used at another time. Most of
the meals consisted of meat of some sort since meat
was the staff of life to the Indians and was always
served generously.

Other foods were served according to the season of
the year. At this time of the year there were wild
potatoes and wild onions with a wide variety of
berries to be either made into sauce or eaten by the
handful as many, especially the children, loved
them best. Bread was made of white camas and
cakes were made of wild berries, crushed while
fresh and dried in little flat patties. Berries were
also dried and made into sauce by merely boiling
them until well done or by leaving them in their
natural state. They were very good this way,
especially the huckleberries. Children loved them.

Sharp rocks were used for all cutting purposes and,
if a family was fortunate enough to have in its
possession a rock in which time and the elements
had worn a hole in the middle, they had a bowl that
had many uses and could be used by all the
neighbors as well, providing they had in their
possession an oblong, round-headed rock with a
long neck or some sort of hand hold on it. This was
the neighborhood grinding machine and at almost

any time of the day you could find someone, young or old, grinding white camas for bread, berries for cakes, or anything that needed to be ground.

Sometimes the bowls were hand made by women who were very patient workers for it took much hard work, determination and perseverance to form a solid rock into a bowl by pounding it in the middle with smaller stones until a hollow in the shape of a bowl was eventually worn into it. But the finished product was well worth the effort and probably gave the owner a feeling of pride and great satisfaction.

As the men finally finished supper they sat around and reviewed over and over the happenings of the day. Some of the stories grew wild and wilder in the telling. Some of the buffalo grew greatly in size as the story tellers told of how they almost hit them with favorite arrows but missed by only a fraction of an inch and, as the young men carried on their story telling with much fun and laughing, the older men joined in by telling of the wild hunting days they had seen in their time which likewise grew more fantastically unbelievable and unreasonable until the young men, with much teasing and joking, finally gave up and listened to their elders who were conceded to be the best story tellers. By numbers of snows they had the most to tell.

After keeping this up for some time a few of them dropped off to sleep while some still quite awake sat cross legged or stretched out full-length on the robes. Some of the older men sat enjoying their pipes which were made of bone or wood and were filled with kinnikinick leaves, which was at that time, and still is, a very popular smoke amongst the older Indians. Kinnikinick is a plant which grows wild in the woods, spreading its thick shiny leaves dotted here and there with bright red berries all over the ground, the leaves keeping their bright green coloring winter and summer.

During all this time, the women were very busy caring for the meat, cutting it up and spreading some of it out over racks built over slow burning fires made of dry cottonwood limbs. Earlier in the evening the men had attended to the hides by spreading them out on the ground as tightly as possible and fastening them down solidly with stakes driven into the ground. When the women had time, they tanned them and let the men have enough strips to make ropes for their ponies.

The women were very particular about their meat. Before they placed it on the racks, made of green willow limbs, they pounded it until it was tender. Then, after leaving it on the racks awhile, they again took it down and pounded it some more. They finished drying it until it was dry enough to keep well.

They did not throw all the bones away, but the best of them were saved for soup. Tomorrow was sure to be a very busy day and soup would not be hard to make and would be a welcome and nourishing food for old and young alike. They would just heat some rocks until they were as hot as they could get. They would put them in a basket made of bark and water proofed, which was already half full of water and meat with plenty of bone added, and instantly the soup would be boiling fiercely.

When the rocks cooled, if the meat was not done to suit the cook, more hot rocks were added or replaced. Those who were lucky enough to have dishes made of buffalo horns, or better yet tin cups salvaged from some battle grounds where they had fought with some other Indian tribe or with white people, were used. Those without dishes, but lucky enough to have spoons made of bone or wood, would gather around the pot and help themselves. What happened to those who had neither dish, nor spoon was anybody's guess.

Occasionally an Indian was fortunate enough to salvage an iron pot or some other cooking utensil from white people who had been unwise enough to wander too far into Indian territory, and these pots and pans were very welcome, especially to the women, who never failed to lord it over their friends and neighbors who had been less fortunate in their raids.

While cutting up the meat for drying, one thing was not forgotten; namely, saving the sinew or gristle. This was pulled out and dried very slowly and laid away for later use when it was stripped in threads and used for sewing. After all the meat and gristle was taken from the shoulders, the shoulder blades were given to the little girls, who were anxiously waiting, and they were soon busily engaged in scraping them clean and dry and then painting and dressing them into delightful little Indian dolls, the dresses being made of buckskin and trimmed on somewhat the same style as their own.

Whenever there was any sewing to be done, the sinew was stripped off into threads fine enough to fit the needle. It was quite strong. It was used for all kinds of sewing such as for making gloves, moccasins, suits for men and dresses for the women and children. Sometimes the thread was colored, with colors taken from different plants or other growths known to the older Indians, and used for trimming. The needles were made of bone and were fashioned to suit the individual, and usually made three cornered, for sewing buckskin.

Now back to the little teepee just on the outer edge of the village. The news of the blessed event was soon related to all the tribe near and far, that the chief's son and wife were the proud parents of a baby daughter. They had named her Owl Eyes as soon as he had returned from his hunting trip, He was quite relieved and very happy. Of course, his first wish was to go and see for himself but he knew that no amount of wheedling, bribing or begging would soften his mother-in-law's heart enough to allow him to get within yards of that little isolated teepee where slumbered the infant child for many days; not until its grandmother gave the husband permission to come and see his wife and child.

CHAPTER II   The Mission

[1]A soft breeze was rustling through the deep
wilderness around a little mission called
Tshimakian which was situated in the beautiful
Spokane Valley in the far west not many miles
from where Grey Cloud and his friends lived. The
people around here were not so war-like as they
had been in days gone by. The Indians did not seem
to want war. They felt that they had been through
enough of that and the few white people who
ventured near them acted as though they felt the
same way.

Occasionally a man who called himself a Priest
called on some of them, and although his actions
were a mystery to them, they did not trouble him
and he did nothing to harm them, except to stir up
their curiosity as to who he was. He did not seem to
fear them as most white people did. He never
carried a gun or even a bow and arrow with which
to protect himself.

But more white people were appearing, people who,
like the priest, seemed to have no fear of them and
wanted nothing but to be allowed to live in peace.
Such were Elkanah and Mary Walker who occupied
the mission house. Nearby stood another cabin, the
home of missionary Rev. Cushing Eells. It was the
first mission some of them had ever seen and they
were naturally curious about it. Some of the trees
had been cut away and a small clearing had been

---

[1] About 1840

made, in the center of which a log cabin had been
built. Around the cabin other improvements had
been made, and a short distance from there stood
the mission itself.

A few yards away could be heard the rippling
waters of the Tshimakian Creek as it wended its
way merrily to join the Spokane River a few miles
distant. (Tshimakian was the first mission in the
Spokane Valley founded by Elkanah Walker and
Cushing Eells in 1838.)

From the direction of the creek, from whose
shadowy depths many a squirming spotted trout
had emerged unwillingly, there came the sound of
millions of frogs, while occasionally the hoot of an
owl came from somewhere among the deep and
heavy bushes that lined both sides of the creek.

It was quiet and peaceful here in the valley, with
green sloping hills on each side, as if to protect
these brave pioneers against the many dangers of
new country. The surrounding woods were full of
wild game, which helped to keep up the food
supply. Also, at the right season, an abundance of
delicious berries grew: strawberries, huckleberries,
and others too numerous to mention.

Their living expense problems would have been
even more simple if only the men could have found
time and inclination to hunt more, and the women
could have had more time to search out and gather
the ripe berries as they grew in their many hiding
places.

But missionaries, wherever situated, found many worries attached to the work they had come so far to do and one of these was the fact that the Indians found it so hard to understand them and their intentions. To make the Indians realize that they were there to help and not to harm them was almost next to impossible and, for this, the missionaries knew the Indians were not to blame.

The Indians could see that these white people were different; that they never tried to cheat them, nor to steal from them and that they were always willing to help them when they needed help.

For this reason, the Indians tried to be good to them, for they often needed help. Quite often they would bring their white friends meat or berries and sometimes they would bring them dried meat or other dried food, such as salmon and camas, which the missionaries were always grateful to receive.

So, in time many of the Indians of this tribe came to realize that the white people were somewhat like themselves, in that some were good and some were bad; but the bad ones were so very bad that their badness so far overshadowed the good in the others that the Indians found it hard to understand just what the good ones were good for. Who were they then and what was it all coming to?

They finally realized that the white missionaries were trying to teach them something; but what? They taught that their God was a spirit. But they believed in a spirit God too, so this had to be explained to them and, until the white people could learn to speak to them in their own language or some of them could learn to speak English, it was impossible to see where they could make any headway. But the missionaries saw these obstacles and it did not take them long to decide on a way to overcome them.

By much patience, determination and hard work they finally mastered enough of the Indian language to give them the respect of these friendly Indians and the ability to speak as man-to-man, with them and thereby enjoy real fellowship with them which was the only way to reach the heart of the Indian and to promote a better understanding.

At first the Indians were very curious about the white missionaries which made it very hard for the women, ventured so far west. In spite of the friendly overtures of the Indian neighbors, at times it became almost intolerable to find that they were so persistently being watched, night and day, whether outside or inside their homes, by men, women and children, whenever an opportunity was offered. They dared not open the door, unless from sheer necessity, for if there were any Indians around they would be sure to crowd into the little cabin, and out would go what little privacy they had been able to enjoy; for if a white woman was lucky enough to have windows in her cabin, it was never private, for the windows would usually be full of dark faces.

The way the white people dressed, lived, worked, cooked and ate was all so fascinating to the Indians that the temptation to watch was overwhelming and if the white people showed too much resentment they would probably have laid it to the fact that they were up to some mischief and could bear a little more watching. Thus, along with learning the language of the Indians, missionaries found that they needed to study their nature also and while the Indians were teaching them their language, they must let them learn the English language along with the ways of a God-fearing, law abiding citizen of America and not to be imitators of those who had no respect for the laws of God and man, and to whom Christianity meant very little. So, in this way a better understanding sprang up between them, although it was far from being perfect.

But some of the Indians were loyal to them in all their troubles and did all they could to help them, while some could not get over being suspicious. These were always on the watch for some sort of treachery, which made it extremely difficult to work with them, especially in times of sickness, for at such times they would usually get their own medicine men and it was always dangerous for any white man to interfere. If the Indian should die while in the hands of a white man it was often impossible for him to explain himself out of the consequences, which were often very severe, even costing the life of the white man and perhaps many others, even though the patient would probably have died much sooner, had he been under the care of the superstitious medicine man.

Helping the Indians to learn about civilization was very much like playing with dynamite and often very discouraging, to say the least. No Indian could forget entirely that, after all, these white people really represented their enemy, so even though the missionaries made good friends among the Indians, the missionaries knew that only one thing was absolutely certain: and that was their promised reward in Heaven for the work they were trying so faithfully to do. They wanted above all else to save precious souls, but God's gift of love was free. They knew they were paying for it, and paying very dearly, in blood, homes and all that life holds most dear.

A few years earlier it would have been much harder for the missionaries but by this time most of the Indians in the far West had become reconciled to their fate, and while many could not find it in their hearts to forgive, some had begun coming to them for help and enlightenment. The grateful abused Indians found it hard to keep on hating people who demanded nothing of them in return for all they so willingly gave in material help, as well as spiritual.

Many of the Indians, some from miles away, came for relief from their mental or bodily suffering and were always made welcome at this little mission and often took great pleasure in returning the kindness. This they did in many ways had it ever become necessary to do so. The Indians would not consent to giving the missionaries up when the missionary board advised the missionaries to move to another location where there were more white people and where there would be more protection against danger from the Cayuse Indians who were on a rampage not many miles away. The Spokanes were a peaceful tribe but when they saw their friends were in danger they fought to protect them and did until the fighting Indians were brought under control before their damaging work reached the missionaries.

But it was not for long. A short time later these good people were transferred to what was considered a much safer location near the west coast to the great sorrow of the Spokane Indians who missed their kind friends very much. They had accomplished more good amongst these people than they had ever realized. The good that they had done reached from there far into the hearts to come since the seeds of Christianity has been sown in some of the hearts of the Indians who never forgot. They had become faithful workers amongst their own people and proved as time passed on that Christianity, when truly accepted and lived by any race of people, no matter what race or nationality, will thrive and never die.

Although it became comparatively peaceful here in the West and the good works of the Priest, who often went from place to place, watching over their widely scattered converts, and bringing into their fold a new one occasionally, and the missionaries who had done so much to scatter the Word of God among the Spokane Indians and other places, there was still much fighting and unrest in other parts the country. The tribe in an attempt to find a way to obtain their old way of life in all its aspects of peace and happiness, was roaming from place to place, hoping to find where white people had not intruded. They had lost their freedom, which was something that they had never been aware of until they no longer possessed it.

But although many young Indian men had given their lives for their country's sake, now the time had come when they knew that it was slowly but surely slipping away from them, and that many more lives would be sacrificed before it was over. But regardless of how black the future looked to them, Grey Cloud and his tribe knew that life must go on and, although the white people had changed their ways to a certain extent, the basic pace of their lives would still remain on a level keel, in that they must still hunt and fish for a living, even though this looking for food was often dangerous and sometimes ended in fighting instead of hunting. But eventually they must bring home food for their families and, in spite of all discouragements, they must raise their families.

So, with war always much too near to them and the effects of it always much too evident, life went on. With the old folks passing on to their happy hunting grounds, babies were born to replace them; babies who always seemed, to the mothers, to be sweeter than the ones before, with their bright eyes and thick, shiny hair, their chubby hands and feet.

It had been a year since little Owl Eyes had come into the little village where lived Grey Cloud and those whom he loved and ruled with an iron hand. They had moved many times during the past year, for no place was safe for long, and now little Owl Eyes had a baby sister and they named her Red Wing. Falling Leaf was very happy these days and very busy. She was finding out that bringing up a baby was quite a responsibility, since she had brought one safely to her first birthday which had been duly celebrated by the whole tribe with much feasting and well wishing.

And now little Red Wing was here. There was only one way to feed a baby so, if for any reason the mother was unable to feed her baby, there was always some obliging friend to help her out, but judging by the looks of her two babies, Falling Leaf was getting along just fine. As for clothes, soft and clean deer hides took care of that, along with the soft down in the birch basket for when fresh down was needed there was always more where that came from.

At first, while the baby was small enough to spend most of its time sleeping, the birch basket was perfectly satisfactory, but as it grew older it naturally became more active and other methods of caring for it were necessary. The mother too had more work to do and less time in which to do it, so the next step in the baby's life was its introduction to the baby board which was made of bark, or a smooth board, if one could possibly be found, cut rounded at both ends, about a foot and a half at one end for the top, and the other end was six or eight inches wide.

The baby boards varied much in size and style. Some were large and were often extravagantly decorated with fringes made from buckskin which was also the material used for covering the board. The board, especially the head, was often very beautifully made, with whatever trimmings the mother found available; sometimes it was shells, thread made from horse hair and beautifully tinted in different colors, or of sinew from a deer and colored. Porcupine quills were another favorite type of trimming. These were quite plentiful and were also used on dresses and for other purposes such as being strung and worn as beads. The large boards were more showy, but were also much more cumbersome and uncomfortable to carry, but the small ones with simple trimming were lighter and easier for the mother to carry on her back, especially while she was busy with her household duties.

In making the baby board, a lot of time and patience was required, for it is not as simple as one would think. First the board is covered with buckskin, the front being cut in two pieces, and the two pieces sewed along the edges to the back piece and extending outward for several inches. Along the edges of these two flaps button holes are made and the flaps are laced together with a buckskin string to form a large pocket. Then the baby is warmly wrapped and placed on the board and snuggly laced up where it invariably goes right off to sleep, with nothing but his little face showing and, if removed from his bed, would cry until safely tucked back in his board again, where it could sleep soundly for hours, perfectly contented. A strong rope or wide strip of buckskin was fastened to each side of the board and the board, baby and all, could be carried on the mother's back. Then while at work, whether at picking berries or in digging roots, the mother often hung the cradle on the limb of a nearby tree where the gentle breeze cooperated by rocking the baby to sleep. As the child grew the lacings could be lengthened and more room made for it until it was big enough to discard the board, often much to the disgust of the baby for it was very hard at first for him to get to sleep without the familiar feel of the baby board to support his little body and to hold him steady.

CHAPTER III   New York to Parts Unknown

About the time the missionaries were at
Tshimakian trying so hard to win the love and
confidence of the Spokane Indians, a young man of
fourteen, who was destined someday to see and
become acquainted with the West and many of its
people, lived in New York. His father was a sea
captain and was part owner of his ship and several
others, so naturally his home was very beautiful for
Captain Perkins was a very well-to-do man. But
Fred, his son, was not in the least interested in the
home, the beautiful city, or in anything it contained
for he was only interested in the things his beloved
father did, and he wanted more than anything to go
to sea with his dad. But, of course, his mother
would not listen to him since he was still a school
boy and there were a number of other reasons too,
such as her great ambition that someday he might
become a very famous doctor in the city she loved
best of all and the only place where she thought her
son could have all the advantages she thought he
deserved. Hers was the great city of New York, the
home of many famous men. But Fred was not
ambitious in that way; he only wanted to be a
sailor, nothing else would do, so one day he made
up his mind that there was nothing in the world
that could stop him. Then came the sad blow that
almost made him change his mind; his beloved
father died far out at sea, and had been given a
sailor's burial. After that terrible tragedy, nothing
was said for some time concerning his desires, so
his mother finally decided that the death of his
father had caused him to change his mind. She

hoped that now he would settle down to his studies and forget all about the silly notion of going to sea.

But Fred had not forgotten, not for a moment, and it was only out of consideration for his widowed mother that he had refrained from mentioning his plans to her. His Uncle Samuel had taken over the ship, which was really a trading vessel, and was doing his best to carry on the work his brother had left unfinished. So, one morning there was a stowaway on board the ship, and when the ship had been several days at sea Fred came out of his hiding place to see if he could find something to eat and came face-to-face with his Uncle Samuel.

He was startled and a little bit ashamed but worst of all he was afraid his uncle would take or send him home, and he knew that if that happened he would only run away again, for he was determined that nothing in the world was going to stop him from following in his father's footsteps. Now his uncle, although showing some surprise at the sudden appearance of his wayward nephew, was not as much surprised as Fred expected him to be for actually his uncle had known for a long time what was in the heart and mind of the lad and had been anticipating this very move.

In fact, he had gone so far as to mention it to his mother. As it turned out, she was not too surprised either, although quite disappointed, when she found the empty room that morning.

After a few words, which made Fred very

uncomfortable and a little bit uneasy, Captain Samuel saw that he had something to eat, then put him to work, as he said: "You want to be a sailor eh? That's fine. You don't want to go to school anymore? You don't want to study to be a doctor and become a great man like your mother wants you to be; you just want to be a sailor? Is that right?"

"Yes, Uncle Samuel. I'm sorry but I'd rather be a sailor than anything else."

" I'm sorry too" his uncle replied thoughtfully, "not only for the sake of your mother, but for your own sake as well. It's not going to be easy, I can tell you that right now, and the worst of it is that I am powerless to help you because every sailor has to begin his career at the foot of the ladder and that means that he has to begin by scrubbing the decks, so get a scrub bucket and rag and get down on your knees for that is the way to scrub decks."

"All right Uncle Samuel!" Fred replied eagerly, for the thought that he was not going to be sent home filled his heart with joy, as he started after a scrub bucket. Soon he returned with the bucket and rag, as he smiled happily.

"Where do I start, Uncle Samuel?" he asked, hardly able to contain himself, he was so happy. Looking at the lad, Captain Samuel smiled a little sadly, as he said "My boy, you have no idea about what you're going into, and I know you are going to be sorry many times but there is nothing that can be done about it now, so from now on you are a sailor boy and there's no backing out until we reach New York again, which will not be for two years at least. During that time, you will have to call me Captain Perkins, not Uncle Samuel. This is for your own advantage; there must be no favoritism shown on board my ship."

Thus, Fred began his new life and as his uncle had warned him, it was not easy by any means, but neither was it monotonous for there was always something to do, although he developed scabs on his knees from kneeling as he scrubbed the decks of the ship, and callouses on his hands from continually shining brass knobs and many other brass fittings on the ship, which he was supposed to keep shining brightly through all kinds of weather. Many a night he went to bed too tired to eat his supper and he knew that, no matter how hard he worked, he was still a flunky and would be doing the same kind of work the next day and for days on end to come.

Sometimes a feeling of homesickness would creep over him but it would not last long, for generally he was too tired to lie awake thinking and before he knew it the sun would be shining once more and he was happy again.

As time went on Fred was advanced to a higher position, and the change was a great relief to him in many ways. For one thing, he was able to see more of his uncle which made him very happy. Now he felt that he might be some help to him for his

uncle was not looking very well and was getting
along in years.

By this time, Fred had learned so much about the
duties of a sailor that there was not much about the
ship with which he was not familiar and no task,
however hard or disagreeable, that he would not
try to do. His uncle was forced to admit that it
would be pretty hard to get along without him.
Sailing the high seas was only one of many duties
of a trading vessel. Another very important duty
was to keep the ship in good condition for a ship in
poor shape was never safe.

A ship on entering a harbor, first had to be
unloaded of its cargo, whether it be silk, coffee, tea,
rubber or mineral, then hauled up to where the
men could work on it. Then all the dirt and
barnacles would be scraped from its sides and it
would be cleaned inside and out. After that it would
be painted until it shone all over like glass. Then it
was ready for another voyage.

They sailed to China and Japan for rice, silk, tea or
anything the natives might have to trade for
American goods; to Brazil for coffee, rubber and
minerals; to Africa for Ivory, to Australia for wool
or whatever they might have to trade. They went to
South America, around Cape Horn to ports along
the coast; to San Francisco to trade for hides or
anything they had there to trade, then up north for
furs. They sometimes circled the world, trading for
anything that would be considered profitable, and
always trading anything they had for gold,

whenever it would be found.

Each ship, as it returned home with its cargo and
entered the Harbor, was treated the same way and
sent out with more trading goods, such as wheat,
wool, cotton or tobacco, returning sometimes in two
years, sometimes longer, loaded with a great
wealth of merchandise. These goods were in turn
traded to American merchants to be sold at retail,
to the public.

Many things happened to make the life of the
young seaman anything but dull. Pirates were
known to be roaming the seas and were very
dangerous. They would never hesitate to kill a
whole crew on ship if it was necessary in order to
steal the cargo, so naturally a trading vessel would
be rich plunder. There was always the danger of
meeting such a ship. One day a strange ship
appeared on the horizon. Fred and the others of the
crew were very much excited and alarmed for,
although they had never run into a pirate ship,
there was always that danger to contend with.
There was no way of telling what sort of ship it was
and when they sent up friendly signals there was
no answer. It looked as though the stranger did not
wish to be friendly. This happened on the
Caribbean Sea where many pirate ships roamed so
it was enough to make them all uneasy. There was
nothing to do but to prepare for a hard battle. They
knew that the Pirates fought with everything they
had and they were determined to do the same thing
for the on-coming ship grew more formidable each
moment, disregarding their signals and showing no

signs of friendliness.

Them something unbelievably miraculous
happened, a loud peal of thunder rent the air
startling the intently watching men as a long
zigzag streak of lightning reached down and struck
the mysterious ship.

Forgetting their fear of the strangers, the men
gasped in horror when the great ship shuddered, as
in mortal agony, then slowly sank before their eyes.
They would have done anything to have been able
to help the doomed ship, but that was impossible
for the storm that followed the death dealing flash
was deafening. The great billows rolled and
tumbled, until Fred and his uncle decided that they
had all they could do to keep their own ship from
sinking.

The storm had come upon them so suddenly that it
had caught them unprepared, and now they were
working desperately to furl the canvas sails, lower
the anchor and prepare to drift until the storm
should wear itself out.

For three days they fought a hurricane, which
made it utterly impossible for them to get near the
spot where they had seen the tragedy. They could
do nothing but wait for the storm to abate, but
when the clouds rolled away showing the bright
warm sunshine to sparkle on the rolling waves,
they were so far off their course that there was
nothing to do about trying to get back. They knew
that trying to locate the grave of the ill-fated ship

would be foolishness and a waste of valuable time, and they were concerned the secret of the mysterious ship went down with its men.

At another time, they thought sure they were about to be sucked into a typhoon. They saw it while it was still some distance away. It seemed to come from the bottom of the ocean and to spread out while reaching towards the black sky, taking with it everything that came within its reach. It was a fearful sight and while they struggled wildly to get ready to meet it, they could not keep their eyes from straying in that direction as they worked madly. Then when it seemed nothing in the world could save them, the huge black menace changed its course exactly as though some great unseen hand had turned it from the ship just when it was ready to strike. "Saved by the skin of yer teeth!" one old sailor murmured, with a sigh of thanksgiving, as the grateful men watched the fearful giant disappear over the horizon.

Fred was growing more and more attached to his work. He thought often of his mother and wished he could see her once more, but he could not do that and be the sailor he wanted to be. He was ambitious to become the captain of a ship someday, but that was a long way off, so he did not let it worry him too much. Besides that, he was reluctant to leave his uncle, who needed him more and more as time went on.

Fred noticed that his uncle seemed to be slowing up and that he was not looking very well lately. This worried him quite a bit because being so far from home, there seemed nothing he could do about it. If only the ship was on its way home instead of going in the opposite direction. He felt that if they were in New York he would have some chance of getting his uncle to see a doctor but, as it was, he could not even get him to listen to anything concerning his health.

Then one sad morning the kind old gentlemen did not wake up at the usual time. Fred, becoming uneasy, hurried to his cabin. There he found that his uncle had passed away during the night. The shock was almost too much for him. How he wished that he had been able to get a doctor for him.

After the funeral, Fred made up his mind that his mother was right after all. He knew now that the world was in need of more doctors. If only he had known how ill his dear uncle was. But there was nothing that he could do for him now and even though he felt so alone, he was glad that he had been able to help him as much as he did. Now since he was not needed anymore, he felt that the best thing he could do was to go back to school and stay with it until he was a full-fledged doctor, but not for anything in the world would he remain and practice in New York. He only wanted to be a doctor for the sake of people who needed him most, people who lived in out of the way places where they could die for want of a little medicine or advice.

But that would not come for some time yet, for the

ship was a long way from home and would not be
going back for many months. In the meantime, he
had work to do that would take them around Cape
Horn and on up to San Francisco where they would
trade merchandise for hides or anything they might
find there which could bring them a good profit.
Fred felt that at least he had enough of sailing and
would be happy to remain on land for the rest of his
life.

CHAPTER IV   Shanghaied!!

One day they found themselves in San Francisco, California. While there, Fred decided to look around a bit as he often heard of the many beautiful spots in the city and this was the first time he had ever been able to stop over long enough to see anything. He soon decided that it was well worth his time for there was much to see; too much, considering what little time he had to spare.

While hurrying along the way trying to take full advantage of what spare time he did have, a strange man accosted him in a friendly manner.

"Enjoying the sights?" he asked, smiling, as he walked along beside him. Fred stopped for a moment, eyeing the stranger questioningly. Then he decided that the man merely wanted to be friendly and, after all, he really could use a friend, so he resumed his walk deciding that he would enjoy the sights much more with someone to see them with.

"Yes," he finally answered, "I find San Francisco a very promising city and with so much lovely scenery around it has a background. I don't doubt that someday it will be one of the most beautiful cities in the world."

The two men visited as they strolled along, until Fred suddenly remembered that he was wandering too far away from the harbor and must begin retracing his steps. "Well" he said, as he held out his hand," I must be getting back. The boys don't know where I am. I am glad I met you and I hope we meet again someday. I'd like very much to spend more time with you, but I must be going." "Don't go yet!" The man pleaded. "Come in and have a drink with me just for friendship sake."

"I don't drink," Fred replied. "But I'll go in just for a moment."

The man led the way into the saloon where he ordered drinks. The man behind the counter looked searchingly at the stranger as he poured something in two glasses and shoved them across the counter.

Fred glanced at the bar tender and decided that he was not a man to be trusted. He was a short squat man with the shiftiest eyes that Fred had ever seen. If only he had gotten the same impression of the good-looking stranger sitting beside him and had not allowed him to lead him into temptation, how different would have been his story. But he was young and boy like, he allowed the stranger to talk him into taking his first drink.

He had never taken a drink in his life, but just to please his new-found friend, he took just a little, but it was enough. He did not know what happened after that, until he awoke and found himself in the dark and filthy cabin on some strange ship. Springing to his feet he rubbed his eyes, unable to believe what he saw. Then, seeing a sailor standing nearby, he turned to him. "What does this mean?" he demanded. The man, who was the dirtiest and most ragged sailor he had ever seen, looked at him with an evil grin on his heavily bearded face. "Shanghaied!" was all he said. It was one of the most dreaded words he had ever heard in any language or in any country. He had often heard of men and even boys being shanghaied but never expected to be one of them.

They can't take me!" he almost shouted in his panic. "I'm in charge of my ship, and I've got to get back."

"Too bad," the man answered quietly, and Fred thought he could detect a note of real sympathy in his voice. "I'm afraid your ship will have to sail without you."

Just then the ragged sailor was called away and Fred was left alone. He hurried up on deck thinking that he might discover some way of escape. But when he looked around, there was nothing but water in sight, great billows of water reaching to the distant horizon in every direction. Fred did not need to wonder just why this had happened to him for he knew that in no other way could he have been induced to go on an expedition of this sort, even if he had been free to accept such a job, for the vessel was a whaler and was owned by outlaws, the captain being a very wicked and vicious man.

Whaling was very dangerous work and most whaling vessels were handled and owned by men who had little or no regard for human life. Not only that, the men were sadly underpaid as well. There was not the incentive of big money to make men willing to risk their lives and their whole futures in one big attempt to get rich quick. Not even the promise of a very exciting time catching the whales could induce enough men to board a whaling vessel voluntarily to make up a crew. Many of the whalers resorted to the Shanghai system.

Fred soon found that the men who owned the ship were very cruel and abusive. He was startled into the full realization that his life and the lives of other captives on board the ship, were to be in the hands of these ruthless men for many months to come.

The captain was never satisfied with anything the men did, no matter how hard they tried to please him. Most of the crew were a lawless thieving lot who needed no excuse whatever to heap every kind of abuse imaginable on the helpless heads of those mostly young fellows like himself, who were new at the job.

Some of the men, Fred soon learned were hardened criminals or outlaws, who were glad to escape the law by hiring out to these outlaw sailors who spent their time whaling so far from civilization that they were seldom caught. But most of them were brought on board the boat by the same method used on him, liquor or dope.

Since the whaling business was so very dangerous and unhealthy, the easiest way to get a full crew was to use the method used on Fred and to keep them ignorant of their predicament until well out to sea where they could either work or die. Then if they were healthy and willing to work they stood a chance of living through the expedition.

Fred was a healthy chap and was very capable in many ways so he did not suffer like many of his comrades. Their troubles were generally his worries too and many a day he spent in grieving over a friend's suffering or death.

The vessel was headed straight for the Bering Strait and in due time it reached its destination. The men were underfed, overworked and discouraged, but most of those who had not already found a resting place at the bottom of the sea were still in fairly good health and a healthy human being is not easily beaten.

In spite of their mutual misery they began eagerly looking forward to the wild excitement of sighting the whales. The thought of catching whales was bound to create a surge of excitement in the lives of any group of men that would lift them out of deepest misery for a time, as they were only human.

When they sighted their first whale, the excitement grew greater by leaps and bounds. Some of the men, those who had been on other expeditions and knew what was to be done, climbed into the boats and with harpoons started out after the whales.

To those who remained on the ship, the whale looked perfectly harmless, but those who knew and were out in the boats were prepared for almost anything. Occasionally one was harpooned and would prove to be a real danger. Such a one would often make a dive for the bottom of the sea and if the men were wise and quick enough, they would cut loose and save themselves. On rare occasions the whale in desperation would turn and by either getting under the boat, or striking it with its mighty tail, would upset it or smash it, drowning many of its pursuers. When a whale was killed, it was hauled to the side of the ship and there it was fastened firmly with stout ropes. Then the men went to work with sharp spades and cut out the blubber along with whatever else was useful for oil or food. The blubber was then placed in large cauldrons or pots and rendered out. After this, the oil was poured into barrels and sealed with wax.

At first the men really enjoyed the excitement, but they soon found that life in any form on a whaling ship was anything but pleasant and that once the whales were caught the fun was all over, for the job of cutting it up and rendering the blubber was hard and uninteresting.

The captain, who was a very large man with coal black hair, small wicked eyes, a fat face and greasy complexion with a heavy black mustache was as heartless as he was ugly. The poor captives were driven from morning until all hours of the night with no time off, except for meals, and very little time for that. They were given very little time for sleep and were always tired.

It was hard, backbreaking work and they were horribly abused if, for any reason, they were unable to do the work allotted to them. If one was so unfortunate as to become ill, he was allowed to suffer unattended for days at a time or until he was well or, if unable to care for himself, he was relieved of his suffering by death. If he were lucky enough to have a friend who could find time to care for him and who was efficient as a doctor and nurse, he was indeed fortunate. Not many had such a friend for this took energy, determination and time. Often the friend might do all that was in his power but it was not enough to save a life.

These whaling vessels never ventured near the shore unless it was necessary or profitable. One reason was the fear of being frozen in the ice while up north and another reason was the captain never trusted his men too near the shore, for he was afraid they might escape from him and leave him without a crew. Either calamity would have been disastrous to him and his partners in crime. In fact, there was nothing more dreaded at sea than to get caught in an ice jam for that could mean certain death to all on board, unless they were fortunate enough to be found and rescued, which would be quite unlikely for an outlaw crew on a whaling expedition was not very popular at any time and rescuing a ship bogged down in the ice was dangerous even when all was normal.

Then too there was the general fear that follows all law breakers... being captured and made to suffer for their sins. Being out on the high seas gave them a feeling of security that could not be found on land.

Fred and the other captive sailors would gladly have risked death on an ice jam or anything else however, in preference to their present circumstances, and would have welcomed a chance, however small, to make a break for freedom.

They were fed blubber three times a day, and that grudgingly, for had they been able to live and work without any food at all their captors would have liked it better. But as that was impossible, the men were fed just enough to keep them working although never free from hunger.

The lack of food variety soon told on the men. Many of them died of scurvy and other diseases for want of the green vegetables and other substantial kinds of food necessary to the health of a human being. No man could live under these conditions for more than eight months of the year at the most.

"Well boys," Fred heard the captain say one day, as he and his men were gloating over their large barrels of whale oil. "We made a great haul this time. If our luck holds out we won't need to make another trip up here unless we want to. We can take what we have earned and live on it the rest of our lives."

"That's right!" came the answer. "We might as well head for home right now. Of course, most of us don't know what home is but at least we can head back to where it ain't so blamed cold. But say! What're we going to do with this bunch of fish bait; we're not going to divide up with them, are we? I say we might as well thrown 'em in the Lake and let 'em drift back to Frisco."

"Naw you don't" the captain answered with a wicked grin. "We can't do that! Whacha think we are, MURDERERS? Of course, they can't expect us to divide up our hard-earned money with them, but if they don't go and die here on our hands, we'll dump 'em out alright, but it will be on land, if we are lucky enough to reach a place to dump them. I think that feeding them to the sharks would be kind of mean, don't you? And besides after all it wouldn't do us any good to feed them to the sharks and it wouldn't do us any harm to turn 'em loose."

Just at that moment there was a loud cry of "FIRE!! FIRE!" Every man grew rigid with fear, then the whole crew as one man was thrown into wild confusion, scattering in every direction as though hunting for a way to escape, and there was none to be found.

Fred glanced hastily at the captain. An exultant feeling possessed him - what he considered just retribution falling on the heads of men who richly deserved it. He saw the faces around him change from the unholy joy they had been exhibiting to the most cowardly, most abject fear that he had ever witnessed on a human face. "Yes" Fred thought as he watched them in disgust. "Like all the cowards, you are brave enough as long as you hold the whip, but take that away from you and you are yellow through and through."

But he and his friends, although badly frightened at the thought of fire so far out at sea, had been too close to death all these weary months to let it really get them down now just when they needed all their strength to fight for their lives. For as far as they were concerned, there was nothing else on board the ship for them to fight for.

All was confusion everywhere onboard the burning ship; for a ship on fire, so far from any shore, is a terrible thing. There is nothing much more terrifying than the cry of "FIRE" under the circumstances. On board ship, far from Land and help, there is nothing more to be dreaded. One poor man, fearing fire more than water, became frantic and jumped overboard, where he drowned before help could reach him.

But the captain, although a wicked degenerate man himself, generally managed to keep his crew well under control in ordinary circumstances, soon made it possible for him to get some order out of the chaos that prevailed around him. He knew very well that it was almost impossible to put out a fire that was already so well started. This one would be an impossibility for the old whaling vessel was well soaked with oil and held many years accumulation of old greasy rags and other rubbish.

It was all they could do to keep the fire down to a smoldering stage, a condition which was constant, and continual watchfulness was very apt to remain the same for weeks, or until they reached a port where the cargo could be unloaded and the fire given full attention.

The captain and his men became gaunt and hollow eyed from loss of sleep and over-work, which made them more heartless and mean than ever. The poor captives bore the brunt of the burden that had been too heavy before the fire and was now almost unbearable. Thus, they sailed for days that ran into weeks; weeks that were a constant nightmare and just when they had given up all hope of ever seeing land again they discovered one morning that they were in sight of the Pacific coast. That did a lot to cheer them up. To their great surprise and joy, they soon found themselves being loaded into boats and heading towards the shore.

It was hard to believe that anything good could possibly happen to them coming from the source from which it came, but happen it did, for the next thing they knew they were being unloaded and told to shift for themselves from then on. Whether the crew thought that they would starve to death anyway, they never knew. Fred whose heart was still kind and generous, hoped that somewhere in the hearts of the hard-hearted captain and his equally hard hearted crew, there was a small streak of kindness and the hope that once on land the stout-hearted boys would make it.

But the why and wherefore of it all did not matter now. They were on land, that was all that mattered. What if they did only have blubber to keep them alive? They had lived on that for a long, long time. They could manage now. But so far as the life on the high seas was concerned, which Fred had so longed for at one time, he was utterly discouraged and disillusioned. He decided right then and there that, if he was fortunate enough to ever reach home alive, he would be through with the sailor's life forever.

They stood or sat watching the sailors row back to the ship, then watched the ship as it sailed further and further away until it began to drop behind the horizon. Then Fred looked up, his face fairly shining with joy; slowly, at first, he was recovering his mental balance. Then suddenly the full realization of their release from their long months of imprisonment struck him and he threw up his arms and shouted wildly.

"WE ARE FREE! FREE!! OH, THANK GOD!!, WE ARE FREE!" He was sobbing and laughing at the same time as he looked at the shining faces of the friends around him, some too weak to stand, lying stretched out full length on the warm sand or sitting with their tired arms supporting their knees, enjoying the grateful warmth of the sun. With joyful tears flowing down their weather-beaten cheeks, all talking at the same time and in every way expressing their gratitude and happiness at their surprise delivery from slavery.

It was very hard to really comprehend, as they looked for the last time at the smoldering ship, thankful that they were not on it, as it sailed slowly in the direction of San Francisco where they knew that the cargo would be unloaded and the fire extinguished; the fire that for weeks had been slowly though steadily destroying the big ship.

The old captain knew that it would be only a few days sailing to San Francisco but that meant many days of walking for the men he had left stranded on shore. Now that he had no more use for them he was glad to be rid of them. He and his men were jubilant. They had hundreds of dollars worth of whale oil in their possession, but not a dollar for the men who had earned it.

As the vessel sailed over the horizon, Fred and his friends heaved a deep sigh of relief. Some of them were sick unto death and all were starving, but all were so happy that nothing else mattered. They felt that they had the whole world on a down-hill pull.

Under Fred's supervision, those who were able went to work and dug holes in the sand a few inches deep, one for each man, for these were to be their beds. Fred made them all lie down in bed and cover themselves up to the chin with the warm sand, and let the friendly sun shine on them with its rays of healing power; for here once more, Fred found his medical knowledge to be a life saver.

After the men were made as comfortable as possible, he managed by hard work because of his weakened condition to get some kelp or what is better known as sea weed, a large brown very healthy leaf used by sailors as food. After giving each man a generous helping, with instructions to eat all they wanted of it, he buried himself beside them and there they lived for many days: eating kelp, sleeping and basking in the warm sunshine, getting up only when it was necessary. Fred kept up the supply of kelp and all grew stronger each day, moving around more each day until they were all well of their ailments and growing anxious to start traveling. The first place of importance was San Francisco, California. Here some of the men were at home and others found work, of which there was plenty. But Fred pushed on with another lad, whose name was Jack Wagner, also from New York. He was a long way from home, broke and very home-sick but full of hope and courage. Best of all he was young and the future looked very encouraging to him. So, he struck out to cross the continent afoot.

They dared not think of the long road ahead of them or else their courage might fail them. So, with a light heart, light packs and lighter pocketbooks, they began their long journey home.

They were lucky some days in catching a ride with people who were going their way, but these rides were generally for a short distance, with occasionally a longer ride which always filled their hearts with renewed courage. Many a time they walked for days and days without seeing a sign of a human being, with miles and miles of beautiful green flower studded landscape stretching out in every direction. These days were rather disheartening, to say the least, and there was nothing to do but keep on walking. To stop was to die.

Occasionally they would come to a settlement where the people would take them in and keep them overnight or longer, which would give them a chance to rest up a bit. This was always a big help to them as they never carried much food with them, one reason being that they never had much to take and another was that they never loaded themselves down with anything that they could possibly get along without. Ordinarily they could find berries or roots to eat, whenever they were forced to stop and find them and occasionally Fred would get a rabbit with his bow and arrows but that was very seldom for, to prepare a rabbit, a fire must be built and smoke could draw Indians.

But one day very unexpectedly, they did run into an Indian camp which was hidden from view in a ravine, where no enemies would be apt to find them. Coming upon them so suddenly they and the Indians were very much surprised. They first started to run, then realized that it would do no good. No use running Fred thought. We couldn't run far anyway, and if they wanted to catch us we wouldn't have a Chinaman's chance of getting away. We might as well go and face the music. Maybe if we are friendly they will be too. It sometimes works that way. They don't look too unfriendly to me and I really think that if we behave ourselves they will too. As they drew near to the group, one of the braves stepped forward and greatly to their relief and much to their surprise addressed them in English, as he held out his hand in a friendly way.

"Welcome to our camp. Rest with us," the Indian said.

"Thanks a lot," Fred eagerly answered. "I could use a little rest, but we can't stay long. We've got a long way to go yet. When we reach the coast, we can take a boat to New York, but that's going to take a lot of walking yet."

"Well come on then" the man replied kindly. "We're just getting ready to have our supper, and if you don't mind our company we would like for you to eat with us. We've got some fresh deer meat that I think you would like."

This sounded very inviting to them for they had not had a decent meal since they started on the whaling expedition and the thought that they were going to have some real meat for supper sounded almost unbelievable to them. The wonderful aroma, drifting from the direction of a huge pot hanging over a briskly burning campfire, was very convincing and they eagerly accepted the invitation.

That night the lad took his blanket out under the stars, as usual. He slept very soundly as he was contented and felt assured that he was in good company. The next thing he knew the sun in all its glory was shining in his eyes to waken him to a brand-new day. The birds were singing merrily and the morning was beautiful and life was good.

After a very good breakfast, which he enjoyed very much and which the Indians enjoyed so much watching him eat, he was ready to start on with his long journey, but the Indians insisted he string along with them as they were traveling that way themselves for some distance.

Fred gladly accepted the invitation and he traveled with them for several weeks. The Indians had plenty of ponies, so Fred was able to travel on horseback a while with them.

They always had plenty of meat of different sorts, which was very good for the undernourished lad. They also had Indian foods such as camas, moss from the trees and wild onions, all crunched together and made into cakes or patties and baked in the oven, which was a hole two or three feet deep in the ground, with hot rocks, over which was a layer of willow twigs covered with leaves. The cakes were placed on the leaves, then more leaves were used to cover them well.

The leaves on top had to be large enough to keep out the dirt which was used on the last covering. After several hours of cooking in this manner, the dirt was carefully removed. Then, the leaves and the cakes were all ready to eat. They were very good and Fred enjoyed them. In fact, he enjoyed all of the food; but there was one that had a rather bitter taste, which was not so popular with him until the Indians told them it was good for him. Then he ate it too. That was called bitter root and was found in many dry rocky places. It was easily located as it had a beautiful blossom and is sometimes called a rock rose.

While traveling one day, one of the Indians became ill. Fred knew what was the matter with the man and he also knew what to do for him. So greatly to the surprise of the Indians, he gathered some roots and made some medicine for the ailing man. This soon had him feeling better and able to travel again. This made Fred more popular than ever with the Indians and a few days later when he reached the parting of the way, the Indians loaded him down with all he could carry of food and anything he could use.

The close companionship between Fred and the Indians was only for a few weeks, but the influence of the friendly feeling which extended between them during this time was to continue throughout the years to come. And the Indians never forgot to praise the white boy who had made medicine out of roots as they did, only in doing so he added to their own knowledge of roots for medicine.

One day, after walking all day, Fred noticed that Jack, who always had been in such a sweat to keep traveling, was lagging behind, that he was pale and looked positively sick. They had been uneasy about Indians all the way, and although had been fortunate in meeting friendly Indians once, it probably would not happen again, and the next ones might be hostile, especially since they were getting close to where hostile tribes were known to roam.

But there was no use to worry about Indians now. Fred could see that Jack was a very sick boy and would not be able to travel very fast from now on... "It's a little early," he said looking back at Jack, "but I think we've walked far enough for one day. Don't you? How about getting ourselves something to eat and getting some rest? You look all fagged out."

Jack looked at his friend, tears stood in his eyes as he replied, "Yes I guess you are right, I don't know what's the matter with me lately. I'm scared to death to slow up, and just as anxious to get home as you are, but it just seems like I can't travel any faster. I guess I'm still feeling the effects of that whaling expedition. I haven't felt just right for a long time. But I didn't say anything because I thought I would get all right after we got off that stinking boat. But now I have a pain in my side that bothers me all the time and won't let me sleep some nights. I suppose it will pass off in time, but that's what I've been thinking for a week or more."

"Why haven't you told me this before?" Fred asked, very much concerned. "I could've made it a little bit easier for you by not walking so fast and maybe we could have gotten it stopped by now. If I only knew what it is that's hurting you, maybe I could do something for you."

Jack looked at Fred, smiling sadly. "You can't help it if you're not a doctor. You can't very well be a sailor and a doctor too."

Fred didn't sleep very well that night, as he was more concerned about his friend than he wished to admit, even to himself. He knew enough about sickness to tell that jack could be a very sick boy, but still not enough to any more than make a guess at what ailed him. "If I had only listened to Mother and taken more interest in what medical training I did get. I might be of some help to Jack now. So far from home too with no doctor or even a white settlement for miles around. What'll I do anyway?"

That night he watched his friend tossing in his sleep and heard him moaning and mumbling restlessly. He felt as helpless as a child and despair filled his aching heart. Finally, Jack raised himself to a sitting position, and put his hand up to his left side, as if to relieve the terrible pain there, while he seemed to be struggling for breath. In desperation Fred sprang to his feet and kneeling down beside the sick boy, took him in his arms, searching the tortured face for some inkling of the truth. "If only I knew of anything that would help you, anything that would relieve that terrible pain, but I wouldn't know what to give you even if I could get it. I have never felt so ignorant and useless in all my life."

"That's all right" Jack replied, smiling bravely. "It's probably just something that will pass off in time. But whatever it is don't let yourself worry about it too much. I'll be all right. No matter what comes. You know we've been ready for whatever might come for a long time, the way our lives have been mixed up for us."

"That's right," Fred answered., "but don't talk that way. You know as well as I do that we are going to get home. You will be feeling better in a day or two and then we'll really make up for lost time. Now let's try to get some sleep. You need it bad. You haven't slept a wink tonight and here it will soon be morning. Try to get some rest now."

From then on, traveling was quite slow and growing slower each day as Jack grew steadily worse. They were many miles from any signs of civilization and with Jack so sick on his hands, Fred grew more fearful of meeting hostile Indians. Fred knew that any Indians they might meet along this strip of country they were now traveling were not apt to be very friendly. If he and his almost helpless friend should fall into their hands, they would never reach home alive. The morning came when Jack was unable to move from his bed, so they were forced to make camp until he was able to travel again, which they sincerely hoped would be very soon. That night Jack quietly passed away leaving Fred so shocked and miserable that he thought he could almost wish that he was gone too. His grief was almost more than he could bear.

"If only I had known what to do," he wailed over and over. "Something! Anything! Poor Jack, to think I let him die without doing a thing for him. The best friend I ever had! I just let him die without knowing a thing to do for him. What am I good for if I couldn't even help the best friend I ever had." Then he looked up and prayed, as he had never prayed before.

"Oh, God in heaven show me what I should do. Let me learn how to heal the sick and how to save lives no matter where I find them. Let this be my life. Thy will be done. Amen."

After Fred had buried his friend in the only way possible, a shallow grave, he said another prayer over him and bidding him goodbye, went sadly on his way. He found that he had never really known just how lonesome a person could get, and he was more anxious than ever to get home. As he travelled, he made plans for the future.

He knew that he could always go back to sailing and make a lot of money, but the only ship he wanted, or ever would want, was a ship to take him to New York, for from now on, his wagon was hitched to a star that reached far up above the world of riches. His mind was made up from here on. His business concerned the healing of precious ailing bodies. Maybe he would never get rich but bodies of people were more dear to him than anything else in the world and he never wanted to see another person suffering for want of help he should be able to give, as long as he lived.

He traveled for many weeks, always headed toward New York. He was willing to do any amount of work, if honorable and he was lucky to be able to pay for much of his transportation that way for, when he had once reached the coast, his worst troubles were over. From there, he got a ride on a ship for most of the way to New York. He was right at home on a ship and found plenty of work to do. In fact, he found so much to do that the captain was reluctant to let him go. But he was done with sailing and no amount of talking or of money could induce him to change his mind. Finally, one day the city of New York came in view in the distance. He closed his eyes in reverence and thanked God for his deliverance.

CHAPTER V   Gold

In the city of Galesburg Illinois in about the year of 1848, there lived a man named John Wynecoop. He owned a small farm on which he managed to make a fair living. The house in which he and his family lived was just a small one, but quite comfortable and well-kept. He had been married about six years and his wife, a pretty young woman with brown hair and eyes, did everything to make home pleasant so they were very happy and contented.

Then came the wonderful news about the West. Many a man had lost his head when the news from the west reached him - "GOLD!!! GOLD!!!" Whole fortunes of gold everywhere. Many were leaving their homes. Some were leaving their families, with wonderful promises, hurrying in herds to join up with some wagon train headed for the west to California, the "Golden State", trying to be amongst the first to reach the booming little town from whence the word that men were getting rich overnight had come.

John heard, and the great hope filled his heart and went to his head. He felt that he must go with the clambering mob of men who had gone wild over the magic promises which were leading them beyond the Rockies, even though it meant deserting his little farm on which he had placed all his hopes, many hours of backbreaking work, and all the money he had ever been able to accumulate. He was busy cutting stove wood when a neighbor brought him the news. "Yes sirree!" the man was saying as John leaned on his axe handle and listened with sparkling eyes to the startling words.

"They say you can pick up gold anywhere out there. And it's nothing at all to pick up gold nuggets as big as your fist without even digging for it! And gold dust!! Why they're carrying that out by the mule back load every day."

" Is that the truth you're telling me?" John asked, unable to believe what he heard.

"That's the honest to goodness truth!" the man answered emphatically. "If you don't believe me, you can go and ask Bud Wilson. He's the man who told me about it."

Then turning, the man started away. "Well so long! "I'm in a hurry! I'm getting ready to start for the west in the morning. Better come along. There's a whole train of wagons going and wild horses couldn't hold me back."

John drove his axe deep into the chopping block and hurried to the house. "Mandy!" he shouted excitedly as he reached the kitchen door where his wife was busy getting dinner. I'm going out west! Out where the ground is paved with gold! Where a man can make his fortune just by picking it up off the ground. Where gold nuggets grow like potatoes and where I can get a mule load of gold dust in one day."

Here he smiled fondly and took his startled wife in

his arms. "Of course, dear, it's not as good as that but I really think it must be pretty good, and a chance like this only comes once in a life time, so I think I should go. It shouldn't take very long even if it is not as good as they say. When I return we'll be rich; RICH do you hear? We'll be rich and able to get all the things we've always wanted.

"But Mandy only smiled sadly." I would rather have you than all the gold in the world. I'm afraid for you away out there amongst those wild Indians. Who would care for you if you should get sick? Who would cook for you and look after you? Where would you find a place to live out in that wild country with its highway men robbers and scalp raising Indians?"

John threw back his head and laughed gaily. "You sure do have an awful poor opinion of the west. I can see that, but don't worry, I think a lot of things we hear, both good and bad, are greatly exaggerated. I'll be back, you'll see, before you even miss me and I'll make up for the time I've been away."

The next morning John joined the men in the wagon train heading west. He was warmly welcomed for it was very important that every wagon train crossing the plains be well provided with plenty of strong able-bodied men in order to be prepared to defend themselves against any enemies they might meet along the way. When they reached the lively little mining town in California, John soon found that the reports he had been hearing were not all mere fairytales, although they had been greatly exaggerated just as he had expected. But there was real gold to be found and lots of it. Men were coming and going steadily, coming empty-handed and some going back the same way, and others with enough gold to make them wildly happy - and to make traveling alone very unsafe. He knew that many of these men would never reach home alive. But it was all in the game.

The new men who arrived were usually pretty green and were feverishly anxious to start digging. They wasted no time in getting their claims staked where they all hoped to find their share of the golden treasure. Some got it, while others went away utterly discouraged, having sunk all they owned into some promising claim which turned out to be worthless. Still others were so unfortunate as to run into some lawless gang, a little smarter than they were, who beat them out of the claim and all they had in it.

John soon found that the town was filled with the greatest assortment of men he had ever seen. Some were good honest men who were trying to get their share of the world's wealth in an honest way. Some cared nothing at all for the rights of others and were determined to get whatever they wanted, no matter what the cost. Here he found men who would shoot a neighbor just to get his gold for the slightest excuse or no excuse at all. Gold to such men was just an inspiration for more lawlessness for very few of them ever used it to any good advantage to themselves or anyone else.

Most of the men who had left their homes in the East were good hard-working men who had been rather unsuccessful at home. The need for money with which to get started in some good paying business found them digging hours at a time, day after day, in the rocks and dirt, until they felt that their backs would break. But most of them did not mind too much. It meant something nice at home for the wife and children.

So, they plodded on, week after week, wading through mud and dirty water, scooping up sand and gravel and washing – washing from morning until night, searching, searching... ever searching for the bright flakes of gold, sometimes becoming suddenly, wildly excited, as the water slowly drained from the pan leaving sand, gravel and... GOLD!!!

Sometimes a man would almost go insane with joy, only to find that all is not gold that glitters.

Such a disappointment was almost more than a man could bear. Occasionally a man would be lucky enough to find a gold nugget. Then the whole Sacramento Valley became awake; providing the news leaked out, which would be unlikely if the finder were wise and if he were smart enough to go about binding his claim so tight that no one could find it and if they did, there was no way of getting it away from him. Claim jumpers were everywhere, always waiting and always ready to catch a lucky miner napping. Sometimes it led to gun-play. Many men were killed just trying to hold on to what belonged to them. That was nothing unusual: life was cheap in the west where everything was new in the thrilling California gold rush days.

The beautiful valley of promises: promises of excitement and plenty of bags full of gold for those who knew how to get it or were lucky enough to keep it afterwards. Still greater promises of golden grain and the luscious fruits in the distant future for those who staked their claims in the rich fertile valley not far from the gold mines.

There were always new men coming to the valley. Sometimes there were women and children but not often, for that was no place for women and children, unless it was in the valley away from the mines. Even then it was far from safe for there they had the hostile Indians to contend with and had no men folks to help them, either white or Indian. The white people were after the land and gold while the Indians were trying to drive them away.

During the gold rush days, it took the stoutest hearted women to leave their homes in the East to help their husbands establish better homes in the West or to get gold with which to build up the homes they were leaving behind.

Many of them did not remain long in the West, unable to stand the hardship, taking the first wagon train back home. John soon came to the conclusion that he had struck the roughest place in the world, and the busiest, even though he decided

that it was the most beautiful place he had ever
seen. He would have liked nothing better than to
have a home in the Sacramento Valley, if only it
were a little more safe for Mandy and the children.

There was more drinking and gambling than he
had ever known. After the miners had worked all
day, they were tired and homesick. Many of them
thought nothing of spending the whole night
carousing and gambling their precious earnings
away, for the saying - "Eat, drink and be merry for
tomorrow you may die."

John soon decided that the stories he had heard
were only fairy tales after all. He often wondered if
he had been foolish in leaving his comfortable home
in search of the glittering gold that always seemed
so elusive to him. He was very glad that Mandy
and the children were safe at home. He had made
up his mind that he would keep right on digging
until he made good. He would never return empty
handed as long as his good health held on, no
matter how long nor how hard he would be obliged
to work.

Every man carried a six shooter or kept a trusty
rifle nearby for immediate use. Even your best
friend might hold you up before morning. Saloons
and gambling houses ran wide open. It was indeed
a free country; every man for himself, for there was
no law worth mentioning west of the Mississippi
River. The only law men recognized in that country
was the best six-shooter and the quickest trigger
finger.

The men who ran the gambling halls used every device imaginable. They cheated in every possible way their scheming minds could invent. They had tricks of every description and many a man was shot for calling a spade a spade, or in other words, telling a man off for cheating when he was caught red-handed.

Many a man who was lucky enough to strike it rich gambled it all away in one night. The men who owned the tables seldom lost, unless they knew by losing a little at just the right time, they would then gain back all they had lost with much more added to it. They were very wise at the game and were there to get the gold by hook or crook, and were not a bit particular about what method they used. One old man who had been beaten out of all he owned, even his mules and camping outfit, exclaimed angrily, "They're as crooked as a dog's hind leg: all of them. They're so crooked that they couldn't sleep straight in bed to save their necks." But still he continued to gamble and the gamblers took I.O.U.'s knowing that he would have more gold tomorrow if he lived that long.

But some of the men saved their gold and finally reached home with it. There was much rejoicing in the homes in the East, while those with gambling tendencies and being unlucky or because of sheer bad luck, never got enough gold ahead to even start back.

John worked there for about a year before he

decided he was not one of the lucky ones. He neither drank nor gambled and he worked hard. He came back home every night with the same thoughts running through his mind "No gold yet: what's the matter with me? I dig every day, in just the same way as the other men do: they find plenty of gold while I find just enough to get by. I never strike it rich like so many do. I'd be better off if I'd have stayed home and tended to my farm."

Finally, he made up his mind to go into partnership with a couple of older men whose luck had been about the same as his own. Here his luck changed, for a few days later John dug up some gold which he found in the bottom of his pan. Of course, they were all wildly excited at first and spent the next few days in working harder than ever, until they were just about played. They knew by then that, even though there was gold there, it was going to be slow and tiring work to get it out. They worked at it for about a year without striking it rich then grew discouraged and decided to sell out. When they got an offer of $75,000, they accepted and divided it evenly amongst them. John started back East. He was glad to get away from the wild West. Now that he had a small stake, he wasn't trusting anyone and the quickest way home was too slow for him.

When he was almost home, he stopped at a town and bought some toys, clothing and everything he could think of to please Mandy and the children.

Then the joyful day arrived: he was home... and

home never seemed so sweet to him! The way he felt right then, he thought he would never want to leave home again.

There was lots of work to be done on the farm, for Mandy had not been able to keep it up as it should have been kept. After so many months of digging in the gold mines, it did not seem too hard and in time he was ready to start work on the house. This was what his heart had been set on from the first. So, before many months, instead of the shabby old house, they had a beautiful modern home and were very proud of it.

Here, with his own father and mother not far off, they lived well enjoying their freedom from worry as long as the gold lasted. It seemed that they could wish for nothing more until John finally realized that their gold had nearly all dwindled away. In fact, he now began to wish that he had remained a while longer in the gold fields for, in spite of all the hardships, danger and loneliness, it was there that he had found gold. The West with its free life and riches had spoiled him and farming on a small farm was too tame for him.

No longer was he satisfied to make a comfortable living; no longer was he contented to remain at home where he could be with his family and where life was, as he once thought, "worth living." The romance of the West, with its roving, fighting Indians, its beautiful scenery, its wild deer and other game, its tall trees and beautiful sunsets, its thriving little towns just beginning to blossom out into beautiful cities and the wonderful feeling of being one of those sturdy men who were helping to show the Golden West off in all its glory.

He realized that he was one of the many builders of the West and the thrill of his experiences there was now a part of him and was not to be denied. The excitement of searching for the elusive gold, although the hardest work he had ever done in his life, had left its mark on his soul. The East could no longer keep him satisfied for the West was beckoning to him and could not be resisted.

CHAPTER VI   Ambition

[2]Needless to say, Mrs. Perkins was overjoyed to see her long-lost son for by now she had given up all hope of ever seeing him alive. His leaving added to the grief of her husband's death and, so soon followed by the death of her brother, had almost killed her.

But she was a very brave woman with plenty of work to keep her busy; work that took her out among the poor people where she found much relief from her own grief by ministering to others in their sufferings and misery, for in well-doing, she found consolation for her own heartaches.

Fred found it very peaceful at home with his mother and enjoyed many happy days with her. But as he gained back his robust health he became restless once more. His mother, noticing the uneasiness of her boy, became worried, for too well she remembered what his restlessness had led to before. She felt as though she could not bear to have him go on another voyage. She had suffered too much and to lose him now would be more than she could stand.

One night she decided that she could stand the suspense no longer. She must know what Fred was planning to do even though there might be more pain than pleasure in the knowing. Watching Fred pacing the floor back-and-forth... back and forth for

---

[2] (1852)

some time and smiling cheerfully whenever his
mother spoke to him, he seemed to comprehend
very little of what she was saying and had his
thoughts many miles away. She said, "Son, I know
you're not happy as you should be here at home and
I wish you would tell me why. Is it because you
have become too attached to the sailor life that you
can't enjoy home life for even for a few weeks?"

Fred stopped pacing for a moment, gazing at his
mother in surprise, then throwing his arms around
her, he laughed gaily as he gave her a big hug. "Not
a bit of it, mother of mine" he said. "I'm going back
to school, know what I mean? I'm really going back
to school, and mind you, I'm back to stay until I
graduate. I'm never going back to sea. I'm through
with the sailor's life forever. I'm going to take up
my studies where I left off and see if I can learn
enough to be a good doctor. In my travels I have
learned that, in this world of sickness and death,
more doctors and fewer sailors are needed."

Mrs. Perkins smiled happily while tears of joy
rolled down her pretty cheeks. Somehow, she
doubted that Fred would stick to school. It was too
good to be true. She felt that there was still a lot in
the heart of her son that she did not know, and if
she did know, she probably would never
understand. She glanced out of the window at the
beautiful garden surrounding the magnificent
mansion, which was "HOME" to her, then around
the luxuriously furnished room in which they were
standing. Poverty was unknown here. Negro slaves
flitted around here and there, ready at a moment's

notice to do her bidding. Anxiously they vied with
each other for the chance to wait upon "young
master" who was clearly beloved by all.

"You are very wise," she answered, smiling as she
kissed him tenderly, "but son, you have been
through so much and have been working so hard.
After all, why should you be always working? It is
so unnecessary for you are a very wealthy young
man. I am glad that you're going back to school
though and now that you have seen so much of the
world I hope you will marry some nice girl and
settle down to enjoy the great wealth you so richly
deserve."

"Gosh mother, not so fast" Fred answered
teasingly. " I want to go to school all right, just as I
said, but I don't ever intend to marry. That's
something I hadn't even figured on. I intend to live
in single blessedness all my life. No sirree, I love
my freedom too well to go and tie myself down that
way, and besides, I could never find a girl in the
world who would be interested in the sort of life I
intend to lead."

"Why Fred," his mother exclaimed. "I cannot think
of anything that would be more interesting than
the life of a doctor's wife."

"Well," Fred grinned, "I guess it would be quite
interesting all right but I'm afraid it would be too
exciting for most girls. At any rate, I expect to be so
busy that I won't have much time for girls. Another
thing, I know of no girls around here that I would

want to be bothered with."

" Why Fred," his mother explained in exasperation.
"How you do talk. There are lots of nice girls
around here. One would think that you were a
regular woman hater."

"Oh, no," Fred hastened to explain as he gave his
mother a big squeeze. "I'm not a woman hater by
any means. I love 'em all. I know that it is true that
there are lots of nice girls here in the big city but,
as far as I know, they are all too to helpless to suit
me. They take up too much of a fellow's time. I
expect to be a very busy man. A wife would only be
a hindrance to me."

At this, his mother laughed merrily and kissing
him fondly said, "That's all right son, have it your
way. You may change your mind someday when
you find the right girl."

The next day Fred went back to school filled with
ambition and a high resolve to make his life
something worthwhile. He studied hard and did
exceedingly well. But true to his word, he left girls
entirely alone for, as he had told his mother, they
did not fit into his scheme of life.

As he progressed in the search for knowledge he
found that, instead of having interfered with his
education, the experience he had gained had
enriched and broadened his mind in a way that
helped him a great deal. He had gone around the
world twice which was an education in itself, and

his knowledge of people of many nationalities was unlimited.

The world to him was not the dark, unexplored, unexplained mystery of the dark ages. It was a glorious moving globe of land and water, a world with ever onward pressing human beings, humans with a goal that reached far beyond the present time: and he was one of them.

He was a fiend for studying and he studied everything that came his way. By hard work he finally received his diploma which indeed brought him the greatest feeling of complete satisfaction he had ever known in his life. He knew that there were many more things he needed to know but he would learn them as time went by.

Needless to say, his mother was highly pleased and gloriously happy. Why shouldn't she be happy, for her boy was all any mother could desire. When he showed her his diploma, her heart was overflowing with happiness and pride. "Now, my son," she said as she placed her hands on his shoulders, her lovely face aglow with the ecstasy that filled her heart, "you will soon be one of the most famous doctors in the city of New York and how proud I shall be of you, my own son."

But Fred smiled knowing what a disappointment he was going to be to his ambitious mother. "No mother, I don't expect to become famous, not where I'm going. While sailing from port to port in my travels over so many parts of the world, I found much sickness and suffering. I came home with the desire to learn more about medicine, not for my own behalf, but for those who need me. New York doesn't need me and to become one of the greatest doctors of New York even if I was conceited enough to believe I was that good, would be the least of my desires."

"Why, Fred" his mother exclaimed, almost angrily. "What good is your hard-earned diploma if you do not intend using it your best advantage? You are capable of going a long way in your chosen profession. Do not disappoint me, my son, by throwing away your talents."

" I'm not going to throw them away, mother," Fred hastened to explain. "I am going to use them to help the poor people who scarcely know what it is to have a doctor, for those who have lived in ignorance; for those who live so far from civilization that God is unknown; who are so ignorant that they grow up by chance or often die young knowing nothing of the life-saving power of education and medicine."

"And do you not call that wasting your talents?" Mrs. Perkins asked impatiently. "Why, Fred, you dare not throw away all you ever earned by all these years of hard work. You must not waste your time, which is so valuable, on those poor ignorant people whom you have never seen and should never associate with. They will pull you down, down to unbelievable depths until you have sunk lower than they are. I know what I'm talking about because I've seen it done."

"And I shall endeavor to lift them higher and higher, to unbelievable heights, to teach them to read and write; how to care for their bodies; and mostly all about God, about how he placed remedies here on earth for the good of the poor as well as the rich. No, mother dear," he continued, "my mind is made up. Your arguments only show me more clearly where my duty lies. Your ideas about climbing up the ladder of fame are right. There is no question about that, but they do not concern me in the least. I'm not an ambitious man, so I shall leave that distinction and honor to those who aspire to it. I'm sorry mother, my field of work lies in the far West where medical aid is badly needed and where a man with a fair education can really use it to the very best advantage. Why I could never do my best work cooped up here in the city. I would feel cramped for space. I must figure out my own line of work and the problem of how to go about it. I must be allowed to go about it my own way."

So once more Mrs. Perkins was forced to give way to a will that was stronger than her own and for a course she considered very unworthy. But this time, deeply hidden in her heart, lay the climax to her great disappointment. The fact that Fred would not use his talents for bringing honor to herself was very detrimental to her pride and she felt that, in following his own inclinations, he was lowering the standards of a family of their financial circumstances. Fred knew that he was going to do the very thing his mother was begging him not to do. He loved her and hated to hurt her but that did not lessen his determination to do what he thought was right.

He had no patience with the wealthy people who made up his circle of friends and he could not bring himself to see his mother's point of view. It looked all wrong to him. To one who had seen so much of the world, New York was only a spot on the map and was overrun with doctors who were working overtime to outdo each other.

He did not care for the competition that was supposed to be the life of trade. He did not care for fame and he did not care for riches, so why worry? There were plenty of others to keep up the fight for that "New York" spot on the map. It was a regular bee hive to him and he did not care to mingle there.

The girls were all alike to him. He liked them all but loved not one. Several of them were a little bit more than interested in him but, if he noticed anything special in the warmth of their smiles, he did not attach any meaning for it. He was too busy getting ready for his journey West to allow anything to hinder him.

His mother pleaded with him gently at times, and sometimes impatiently. Fred only patted her on the shoulder and smiled, not wanting to start another dispute which never got them anywhere. But one day she refused to put it off any longer and demanded a satisfactory answer.

"What do you think will be gained by you giving up
all your friends, your home and the chances of
making a name for yourself here in New York, and
going out there to live amongst the wild Indians
and the wolves? You could die way out there and no
one would be the wiser because we would never
even know where you were."

Fred only smiled as he held his mother's soft hands
in his. "This is a way that I must go; God planned it
all for me. It leads to far off lands I know: the West;
my life, and my destiny," he gently answered as he
kissed her and went out in the sunshine leaving
her to figure out just what he meant.

CHAPTER VII   Out West

One day Fred started west with a government commission in his pocket. It had been no trouble at all to get the commission, for white men, especially doctors, were badly needed out there. He was acquainted with some of the Hudson's Bay trading company men and planned to make good use of their forts, which were strung all along the trail he would take, and he knew that he would be able to travel in comparative safety that way.

The forts were built strong enough to resist any attack, however vicious, made by fighting Indians or other enemies. They were made of heavy logs fastened together so closely that the only openings were the small holes made just large enough to hold a gun barrel.

The men at the forts were traders or merchants who traded merchandise for either gold or furs, mostly furs. Their furs usually brought good prices so the traders did very well at the business. This was especially true when trading with the Indians for very few of them knew the real value of their furs and the traders got them for practically nothing.

As a rule, these men got along very well with the Indians but occasionally a band would go on the war path. The white man never knew just where the Indians would strike next. The traders learned to always be prepared for the worst so the forts were built strong enough and arranged in a way to resist the Indian attacks, no matter how great the surprise.

Naturally, as so much depended on the number of men stationed at the forts, Fred's request that he be allowed to join them whenever his journey east or west led him near one of the forts was eagerly accepted.

The Hudson's Bay Company constantly had men on the trail from the East to the West, and consequently they met and dealt with many different tribes of Indians. Some were quarrelsome and others were quite friendly.

It was impossible to maintain peace at all times. The war-like Indians always had plenty of grievances which they were apt to air almost any time. Grey Cloud and many others of the same mind cared very little whether the party they were attacking were friend or foe. They were white people and that was all that mattered. The men soon found Fred almost indispensable, for besides being very capable, he was one of those most willing and trustworthy men. He spent much of his time traveling alone, independent of any help other than that of one or two companions, who like himself would rather travel alone and do as they pleased.

Owing to his many months' experience as a trader while sailing from port to port, he was a valuable man. His fine education made him an important figure in all business dealings. In an emergency, he would cook their meals. Amongst all his accomplishments, the one that made him the most popular to these men with the fact that he was a good cook.

Anyone needing medical aid always received his undivided attention. Fortunate indeed was the man who, when becoming ill so many miles away from civilization, injuring himself in any way or getting a bad toothache, found himself near "Doc", as they called him. Fred was fortunate in being able to avoid any fighting with the Indians. It happened that he was never obliged to be in a war. He would never have hesitated to fight if he or anyone else had been in danger. However, this fact did not worry him in the least. He did not care to be in a war in any way and he would have gladly helped an Indian as well as a white man if one were in trouble and needed him. To him, they were all human.

As he traveled farther West he saw more Indians and less white men, and white women were almost a curiosity. Occasionally, he would meet a white man who was married to an Indian woman. At first this surprised and even shocked him. He gradually grew accustomed to seeing them and in time he could think of many reasons for the white men marrying Indian girls. He found that white men, lonely and tired of living alone, really learned to care for the little Indian girls and married them for love. In time, it became a very common thing to see a white man settled in a comfortable log cabin with an Indian wife and several little brown, grey or black eyed children peeping out from behind their mother's buckskin skirts. Their women were generally friendly and treated him well. He appreciated this very much and, when needed, he helped them in their times of illness, often saving a life. For this reason, he was highly respected by the white people, and was seldom troubled much by the Indians, unless it was in his travels further East, where he was only a white man. But those who knew him better soon came to the conclusion that he was one white man who wanted nothing but to be friendly, and was allowed to live amongst them and be of help to them.

In his work, he was obliged to travel back and forth from the western part of the states to the middle states. Most of the time he went on horseback with pack horses to carry luggage, for there were few wagon roads over the country which he traveled. In some places, it was all he and his companions could to do to get through with their horses. Their packs were often rather large and heavy, causing the packs to catch onto the trees and bushes as they passed through.

Whenever they came to a river which must be crossed, they would either ford, swim or cross on a raft. This was generally risky and sometimes dangerous, especially if the man with whom Fred was traveling happened to be a fur trader and had a heavy load of trading goods with him. Often in the springtime the small streams were swollen and full of debris of every description, besides being deep and full of dangerous undercurrents which would often carry away a valuable animal or a whole raft load of goods.

The raft was usually made of any long poles that could be found along the banks of the stream. After they were hauled or carried down to the river bank, they were nailed or tied together to form a stout platform on which the pack sacks were piled. Then the raft was poled loose from the banks, pushed by the poles or paddled across the stream if the water was too deep for the poles. Horses were walked across the stream unless it was too deep, in which case they had to swim.

Sometimes the traveling was not bad but at other times it was very disagreeable and Fred was obliged to suffer many hardships. Being on horseback and when canoeing, which they sometimes did when the lay of the country permitted, they had very little protection against the weather. A heavy canvas was used for a shelter at night against rain or snow. Whether good or bad, the weather never hindered them very much. Wild animals were plentiful all along the way. They seldom troubled anyone unless they were starving or forced to fight in self-defense. Then came the constant danger of sickness. Being exposed to all sorts of weather, they were never quite free from the fear of getting sick.

But their worst fear of all was that of being attacked by the Indians. Of this fear, they were never entirely free, for there were always bands of Indians roaming the country in places where they were least expected, stealing anything they could lay their hands on or could carry away. From a man's hat to his best horse, Grey Cloud seldom missed a chance to be among the raiders for he was always scouting for luckless white people.

Fred always rode good horses and he had one animal that he prized a lot. One morning, just when it was darkest, he and others with him were awakened by the sound of running horses. Seizing their guns, the men hurried out just in time to hear the familiar sounds receding in the distance. They knew that once more the Indians had sneaked up on them in the dark and stolen their horses.

Fred hurried out to see if they had taken his pet or favorite animal and to his sorrow the horse was nowhere in sight. But some of the others were still there, which was some consolation, for at least they were not afoot. By the time the horses were caught, it was getting light enough to see which way the raiders had gone. The Indians had often admired Fred's horse. It was coal black and was always ridden by the same man. Fred had surmised this for he had often heard of the Indians great love for black horses. It did not take him long to figure out who the guilty Indians were, especially since Grey Cloud was becoming so well known amongst the white people.

To their great surprise, they had not gone far when they spied the Indians and one especially who, although an expert horseman, was still trying desperately to get astride the plunging horse. The animal was afraid of Indians at any time and he especially did not relish the idea of being handled so unceremoniously so early in the morning. The other Indians, becoming frightened, were soon disappearing over the hills leaving the struggling horseback rider to his fate. But the Indian was stubborn and was determined to have his prize. He had lost horses to the whites and felt that turnabout was fair play. Fred and the other men took out after him just as the Indian managed to get astride the wildly excited horse. Seeing that he was about to be caught, the Indian jabbed his heels into the flanks of the bucking, plunging animal and managed to turn his head towards the Missouri River only a few yards distant. In a moment, Fred saw what his intentions were. It was too late to stop him and into the wide deep water the terrified animal plunged, the Indian hanging onto his mane. There was nothing to be done about it; for if they tried to shoot the thief, there was great danger of shooting the horse. As he climbed up the bank on the other side of the river, Fred sighed for he was sure he would never see his horse again although he was always on the watch for him whenever there were Indians. But once more, the young Indian had won. Perhaps he thought the beautiful horse would help him to forget some of the prizes he had lost to the white people.

The now badly crippled cavalcade journeyed until it reached the fort that was their destination. Here they left their weary horses, for they decided to go on in canoes, as they sometimes did whenever it was at all feasible. This depended on weather, time of year or on whether they were going up or down the river.

By canoe, they knew that it would only take them a few days to reach the next stop. There, if necessary, they would get more horses. They were soon floating down the Missouri River which like most rivers has many moods. Sometimes the going was smooth and peaceful, paddling was quiet and restful. Often it was so swift and rough that it taxed them to the limit to make any headway at all. Occasionally, it was so bad that they were forced to take their packs and canoes on their backs and walk or climb until they reached better going. Then at times the climbing was so steep and rocky that they had all they could do to reach the top. Whenever the weather was bad this canoeing was anything but pleasant. They were not traveling in the winter so they escaped most of the real cold freezing weather. They finally reached the fort and, after spending a few days there, they found some horses and started back West. This of course was in the summertime so Fred enjoyed it immensely. He was a lover of nature and the scenery along the way was quite changeable and very beautiful.

They traveled miles and miles through wild unbroken country, not a sign of human life for days at a time. Sometimes there would be miles of rolling prairie land stretching out on every side, covered with green bunch grass, with occasionally a large herd of buffalo to break the monotony or a bunch of prairie birds fluttering out of sight. Everywhere were beautiful flowers blooming in great profusion, as though glorying in the fact that man in his wild scramble for more land and more riches had not yet discovered their hiding places.

Then they would travel through heavy timber land with giant trees towering majestically above them where no man had ever laid an axe and wild animals roamed unafraid. He loved the scent of the pines, and the huge trees swaying gently in the breeze were a constant source of enjoyment to him.

Nature paints a beautiful picture when allowed full sway, unhampered by man. Fred stood spell-bound gazing at the magnificent country spread out before him, wondering how long it would be before man with his many weapons would destroy it all; man, who was trying to make it over to his own liking to suit his craving for more riches, more power, more property, more of what God in His loving kindness was freely giving to them, in its wild and beautiful state to do with as they pleased.

For those who cared for sports, there was plenty of game with no game laws attached and fishing was always a source of great enjoyment for some, but Fred enjoyed no sport that required taking a life whether it be man or beast.

Whenever they grew tired of traveling, they would find a nice spot for a camp with plenty of grass and water for the horses. With stars shining above them and perhaps a round, beautiful moon hovering over them as if to remind them that it had been shining in the same way for many centuries, they would spend the night. Early morning would find them preparing for another day's journey.

They were traveling by water. It was no trouble at all to pull the boats up on the banks of the river and unload their camping outfits for the night. Getting started on the way in the morning was much simpler this way.

The route they usually took led them to Missoula, Montana. From there they went through Eagle Pass to Spokane, which by the way was not much more than a settlement at that time. Then they went across country to what later became Marcus, Washington. Soon they were at the old fort called "McDonald's Block House."

Here Fred remained for a while for this was the fort to which he had been sent and where he usually made his headquarters. Besides that, he liked the peace very much. He would have liked very much to have been allowed to make this his permanent residence but instead he was sent right back over the trail he had just traveled with more important papers. He had a young man with him this time. The Indians were growing suspicion of their actions for they feared the two white men were messengers of war. They would have killed them before giving them a chance to leave had they dared, but the men at the fort were continually on the watch out for any disorder so the two managed to get away without any trouble. As a rule, Fred had no trouble in making friends with the Indians. They found it rather hard to be unfriendly with a man who always met them with an outstretched hand and smiling face. Besides, he was always ready and willing to help any who were in need of help no matter what their nationality might be.

But this did not always give Fred the protection that he needed. Although the Indians accepted his help with smiles of satisfaction, many of them were still his enemy at heart. They felt, and with good reason, that no white man could be trusted, especially if he worked for the government.

Suspicion that he had papers with orders that he deliver them at some distant fort caused the Indians to feel that he was not the friend that he pretended to be and many of them would gladly have stuck a knife in his back or taken a pot-shot at him from behind some tree if only they had dared.

But in spite of everything, Fred and his partner made good time for the first few days. Then one morning when they awoke they saw their horses were gone. They could tell by the moccasin tracks that the thieves were Indians.

They were now in a very bad predicament. He knew the papers he carried may have been the incentive for the robbery but they still had them and this puzzled him a great deal. It began to look as though the Indians had just wanted their horses or were merely trying to torment them. But his partner, a tall lanky fellow named John Hill whose long yellow hair was badly in need of a pair of shears, explained it this way: "I'll bet your bottom dollar that we're alive today because the Indians are superstitious about killing people when it's dark. They think that if they kill people during the night their spirits will hang around and haunt them."

Fred laughed, "Well, I'm glad that they feel that way about it but that's not going to keep them from coming back today and I'm not afraid to say I'm scared. I've seen some tough times in my life, but anything is better than being tortured by those red skins!" He glanced fearfully around, then looked ruefully at their pack sacks. "We've got to keep going, but what are we going to do with all this luggage to carry? Those Indians know we can't carry all that stuff and that we wouldn't live long without it. It looks as though they intend to let us linger on a while knowing they'll catch us again before we get very far and it gets dark. No matter how fast we walk, we couldn't get far and there is no use trying to hide. I think the only thing we can do is try and outsmart them. If they were too superstitious to kill us when they had us dead to rights, it could be that we could figure out a way to fool them. At least it would be worth a try. If we could just string them along until we reach the Missouri River, we might make a getaway. Of course, there's the chance that they have what they are after, the horses, but we can't afford to take any more chances than we have to. Besides, I can't imagine them leaving us with all these groceries. What puzzles me is why they left them at all. It must be that they were not hungry but, whatever it was, we're alive. That's what matters. Now we've got to figure out some way to stay that way - and fast!"

Just then Fred glanced up and seemed to freeze in his tracks, for there, sneaking from tree to tree a few yards away was an Indian. For a moment, he thought he could feel the hair standing up on his head and the tingling of every nerve in his body; but with an effort he controlled himself for he knew their lives were hanging in the balance.

"You know how superstitious they are: well, we're just a couple of guys gone loony. That shouldn't be too difficult, under the circumstances, and I think we can scare them away. It's our only chance."

Glancing up cautiously, Fred could see in the distance figures darting here and there, from tree to tree, making signs that he could read. He knew by the signs and maneuvers that they wanted to catch them alive. To the savages this meant much more entertainment and more excitement and to the unfortunate victims, if they should be caught, more torture. But the thought of being taken alive and literally being torn to pieces by these bloodthirsty red skins only made the men more desperate and determined to escape. Fred ventured another glance and saw that the woods were full of dodging, feathered heads, with here and there a shiny, greasy, painted body glistening in the hot sun for an instant.

Suddenly Fred gave an unearthly yell and, springing at John, flung his arms around him and

threw him heavily to the ground where he
pretended to be trying to choke the life out of him.
John jerked away from him, his long yellow hair
streaming down into his eyes, his large white teeth
gleaming in the sun. Growling like a bear, he
clawed and bit at Fred as the two men fought and
rolled all over the ground.

Just as the Indians, out of curiosity, began drawing
a little nearer, Fred seemed suddenly to forget all
about the fight and springing to his feet, snatched
his hat from the ground where it had fallen and
began cutting it to pieces with his knife. He tore
and cut until it hung in shreds while he danced
around growling and screaming the whole time.
Then he slapped it back onto his head and looked
around grinning for all the world like a man gone
stark mad.

"You heap crazy!" John yelled, as he grabbed his
own hat and began cutting it just as Fred had done.

"Me heap Big Bear!" Fred replied as he dropped
down on his knees and started trotting after him.
They circled around this way for a few moments,
then finding that their heavy packs which were
fastened onto their backs made it impossible to
keep up the pace much longer, they began rolling
over and over onto them, growling, kicking and
clawing until they broke loose from them.

Then grabbing the packs, they tore them open and
scattered the contents all over the ground,
devouring great mouthfuls in the meantime.

Suddenly Fred sprang to his feet, pretending that he had just discovered that they had an audience who, edging nearer and nearer in their curiosity about the strange actions of the two men, stood quite nearby and in plain sight.

"Ugh! Me heap big Injin!" he exclaimed as he ducked his head and, with a very good imitation of an Indian war whoop, began dancing and prancing around in regular Indian style. John doing the best he could to follow suit.

By this time they were both perspiring and covered with dirt. Streaks of dirty water ran down their faces, their hair matted, sticky with dirt hanging in their eyes and over their ears, made their actions look very realistic indeed.

"Me heap big Injin!" Fred repeated, as he turned and started towards the stupefied Indians. "Me heap Big Chief," then with outstretched hands of welcome he started towards the Indians. This was too much for the bewildered savages and, turning, they fled wildly through the woods.

The two men followed closely for a short distance, running leaping and yelling savagely, singing and growling in turns and cutting all kinds of capers. In short, doing anything that would keep the Indians running the opposite direction. Finally, they decided that for the time being they were safe, although, knowing the Indians as he did, Fred knew that their chances of living through this day would be pretty slim. So, they kept up the antics for the rest of the day, fearing that some of the Indians may have lingered nearby to reassure themselves that the white men were not making fools of them or that some of the Indians would return just when they were not on guard and would be hiding behind the trees.

Finally, the two desperate men concluded that by the way the red skins were traveling, they must be some distance away. They decided to take a chance on some of the brave ones remaining behind to keep a watch on them and returned to their packs to try and make a get-away. Very cautiously they gathered up their scattered belongings, while purposely, to convince the Indians that they must really be crazy, left some goods which of were real value and hastily stuffed the rest of them in their pack sacks and hurried away, as common sense allowed them to. Since they knew that they must still be very careful, they kept up their insane antics for the rest of the day.

"We sure fooled them!" John exclaimed jubilantly as he made ready to let out a terrible screech that echoed far and long through the woods.

"I guess we did," Fred replied. "We just about scared the daylights out of them. I hope they stay that way from now on. It makes my scalp tingle every time I think of them. You know something? It wasn't hard for me to act crazy. I wasn't fooling a bit. I was simply scared crazy and that's no joke. I was never more scared in my life."

Both men knew that the only hope of reaching the fort alive was in keeping the Indians deceived, so they kept at their performing, even after the enemy must be many miles away. Thus, the next day, when a small band of the tribe drew near just to make sure of these men who seemed to be full of devils, they found them down on their hands and knees growling at each other and eating grass. They ventured no nearer, but turned and fled, not knowing that Fred had been watching and had spied them first.

In spite of their superstition, the Indians became so curious that they later returned once more. Some of the more reckless of them ventured near enough to speak to the two desperate but seemingly fearless men. Instantly Fred and John both sprang to their feet and rushed forward to meet the Indians, gesturing and jabbering wildly, as though overjoyed to see them once more.

This was too much for the nervous Indians. Crazy or not they could see no sense or pleasure in capturing or killing two white men who acted as if they wanted to be caught. So once more the Indians turned and fled wildly into the woods living them in peace.

In a few days, the two weary men reached the fort where they recounted their hair-raising experiences, much to the amusement of the men who were stationed there. Anything that happened outside the fort was news to them and was always a bit of refreshing release.

Fred was glad to be relieved of the papers, which he supposed had been the cause so much trouble to them, but his pleasure was short lived. They were almost immediately trusted with more important papers to be delivered to the men whose message they had just delivered.

They rested a few days, then once more they were ready to venture out into the wilderness where death lurked around every bend of the river and where every tree large enough to hide a man spelled danger. Men could disappear from the land of the living as completely as though swallowed up by the earth.

Needless to say, they did not travel the same route every time, in the hope that travelling would be safer that way. Fred was sent on several trips back and forth with important dispatches and, although he never felt entirely safe from hostile Indian tribes on the war path, he was fortunate in never having any more trouble with them. He never failed to get through a message and was proud to be able to say that he had never yet been forced to take a human life.

In his travels here and there over the states, especially along the Missouri river and through the more thickly settled Indian territory, he often stopped overnight with priests who were stationed at the little missions along the way. Sometimes these priests were quite poor with very little to offer in the way of food or other accommodations,

but Fred was always welcome to stay and share
with them what little they did have.

At one of the missions the old priest had only bread
made from wheat he had grown and ground in a
hand mill of his own manufacturing and
homegrown radishes. Another priest served black
birds and that was all. But the birds were well
cooked and were good. This was before the Indians
had become reconciled to the idea of having white
people, even priests, in the country.

After the Indians had become acquainted with the
priests, who were trying so hard to be friendly with
them, the Indians accepted their friendship for
what it was worth to them. From then on, the
Indians brought them fish, venison or whatever
they happened to have or could get. This pleased
the priests very much and after that there was a
more friendly feeling between many of the Indians
and the priests. There was much more food for the
priests who seldom went hungry.

There was a little old log barn on the banks of the
Little Spokane River, at what later became
Spokane House, where lived an old priest. Fred
spent many a night there with the priest in the
little log cabin which stood nearby. Fred managed
to keep hay in the barn for his horse and when
night came he would sleep on the hay and be near
the horse. After he would get his horse settled down
for the night he generally went over to visit the
priest and would often spend much of the night
visiting. The lonely old man was always glad to see

him and to learn of some of the things that were happening in the world from which he was now so widely separated.

The old barn was full of cracks and was far from comfortable whenever the weather was cold but it was shelter for Fred and his horse and he was very thankful for it. In the summer time, it was very nice and since he travelled so little during the winter time, he spent many a night in it.

Spokane house was situated in a lovely spot not far from what later was the city of Spokane falls. Fred loved to sit on the banks of the Little Spokane River and enjoyed the beautiful scenery, while below him in the rippling water, he could see and hear the fish jumping and splashing.

Occasionally a large speckled trout would cause him to smile in admiration as it made a beautiful curve through the air while jumping for flies. But although he loved to watch them, he never cared to catch them. To tell the truth, he was no sportsman. Fred spent much time at Marcus, a small town on the banks of the Columbia River.

Fred often longed for the time when he would be able to start up a little school. He could see a great need there but yet his cause seemed hopeless. He knew that he must have the confidence of the people or else his school would be a waste of time and energy.

One day he was standing on the banks of the

Columbia River watching some Indian children playing in the water when suddenly he heard a scream. Looking up the he saw that a canoe had overturned and several children were floundering around in the deep water. Most of the Indian children who lived along the river banks could swim and usually thought nothing of a good ducking, but Fred saw at a glance that something was seriously wrong this time.

One of the boys ran down the bank and dove out into the deep water. Hurrying up to where the greatly excited children stood watching from the bank, Fred saw the boy come to the surface with a little girl in his arms. He struck out for the shore, swimming hard against the swift current and when he reached the shore it looked for a while as if there was no life left in the little body. Immediately a sad wail of death filled the air. Fred was horrified as he realized that the people had already given the little girl up for dead. Hastily throwing off his coat, he grasped the limp little form in his arms and began administering first aid treatment. He worked with every ounce of strength he had in his strong young body.

Finally, a faint sigh escaped the blue lips. Frantically Fred strove to encourage the small spark of life that had shown itself, a feeling of great joy and thankfulness to God tugging at his heart. In a surprisingly short time the little girl opened her eyes and smiled at him. "Ah! What a relief!"

Fred soon had her wrapped in warm blankets and

carried her to her home where she was given every care under the happy young doctor. In a few hours, she was out playing again just as though nothing had happened. No, not exactly! For now, whenever Fred went in that settlement and for miles around, he was met with smiles from the Indians who had such a short while ago eyed him with hatred and suspicion.

Now he knew that he could soon begin plans for the fulfillment of one of his great ambitions - his beloved school for Indians and white children alike.

But the time was not yet. There was much to be done in this big country and he chafed under the heavy yoke of waiting, always waiting. The people were becoming more friendly but he was still traveling a lot, from place to place or fort to fort, always waiting and watching for an opening for his school or a place where he could set up some sort of a permanent building in which he could practice medicine. Fred kept in touch with his mother and she wrote occasionally but it took months for a letter to travel from the East to the West. Often a letter would be days in the post office waiting for him to return from some distant fort. So, it was after the Civil War was in full swing that Fred learned about the war between the North and South among the white people of the states. Those in the Northwest, unless immediately concerned in it, did not worry too much about it.

Fred received a letter from his mother telling of George who was fighting in the South with Roy.

Both were married to southern girls, and of Joe who was a Yankee.

Fred's sympathies were with Joe and his cause for he wished to see the day that all people would be equal, regardless of nationality or color.

CHAPTER VIII   Wagon Trains

This was in 1859 or 1860, back in Galesburg, Illinois. John Wynecoop grasped his father's hand warmly while tears stood in his blue eyes.

"Goodbye, Dad, "he was saying, "be good and take care of yourself."

Then he turned to kiss the sweet woman who was vainly trying to keep back the tears that were determined to roll down her cheeks and said, "Goodbye, Mother. I hate to leave you this way but we will be back. By that time, we will be able to persuade you folks to go West too."

"I only hope you are right," his father answered. "I only hope you will never be sorry that you gave up all you had here for the West. I can't help feeling that you are making a serious mistake. I'm growing old and I think a lot of my old home, so don't pay any attention to me, Son; maybe you are right after all." The old man pulled out his handkerchief and wiped his eyes as he continued, "Don't work too hard. Take good care of Mandy and the children. That is a big country out there and it would take a lot of people to do all the work there is to do out there, so don't try to do it all by yourself."

John laughed as he placed his arm around his Father's shoulder. "Don't worry about us, Dad. That's a grand country out there. I learned a lot while I was out there and you know I did not come back empty handed. I may not get gold this time but I may get something far better. I know where I can get plenty of land. It is better than the land in this part of the country and I can get it for nothing."

"I'm going to play Injin when I get out there!" little four-year-old Curtis chimed in excitedly, "and maybe I'll see some real Injins too, some with feathers in their hair and all striped too but... Mama says I can't play with real ones," he added remorsefully. Then his face brightened as he continued excitedly, "but I can though, can't I Grandma, if I don't play too rough?"

At this they all laughed, that is all except Grandma.

"Why, Curtis," she gasped. "you wouldn't want to really play with Indian children, would you?"

"I like to play Injin," Curtis declared, and real Injins would know how better than I do!"

"I suppose they would," his grandmother answered nervously, "but I really think you'd better mind what your mother tells you. For my part I hope you never even see one. It makes me nervous just to think of it."

"But, Grandma," the small boy persisted, "God made Injins too, didn't He?"

"Yes, of course," came the reply as she kissed him
fondly over and over. "Of course he did, dear and
may He bless and keep you while you are away out
there. Be a good boy and make Mama and Daddy
write to Grandma and Grandpa sometime, and you
write too, dear - often."

To the old folks, it was a sad parting for too well
they knew that very few who went out West ever
returned. They watched longingly the tearful faces
peering out from under the canvas wagon tops of
the covered wagons as they moved slowly down the
dusty road. With handkerchiefs fluttering wildly,
the cavalcade finally disappeared around a bend in
the road as it began its long journey across the
plains.

John and Mandy had lived all their lives in
Galesburg, Illinois and now with their five children
they were starting out on their great adventure.
With their lovely home, they would have been
satisfied to remain there the rest of their lives but
John was ambitious and couldn't be satisfied with
such a small place. Since he had been out west in
1849 the West with its wide-open spaces had been
beckoning to him and he could not resist.

There were hundreds of acres of the best land in
the world with enough pasture to graze thousands
of head of cattle. Great herds of buffalo ran wild
eating off the pasture which John thought should
be put to better use. A man could raise his own feed
for his stock and plenty of grain for home use. It
was waiting for someone ambitious or brave enough

to go out and stake a homestead.

There was gold and silver in the ground and he thought there should be golden grain on top with orchards and vegetable gardens everywhere. Every man was still a law unto himself and could profit by all these advantages providing someone stronger or quicker on the draw than he did not take it away from him.

The great wilderness provided logs or wood for building purposes. Many men became wealthy in a short time. Best of all it was where a man knew freedom in every sense of the word "The Land of the Free!" What a glorious name!

Although John was anxious to get started, it had taken weeks to get ready. There was the home to dispose of, a task which caused Mandy to steadily wipe away tears. There was money to raise before they could buy the equipment necessary for such an expedition.

It was not safe for one family to venture very far west alone so they must prepare to travel by wagon train. The more families they could get to travel together the better they were protected against Indians. Many tribes were still very hostile. For people foolish enough to venture out unprepared for attack was plain suicide. It usually took many weeks to prepare for such a journey for it was not very easy to get enough families together for a wagon train. It took time for each family to decide to move and then to get ready. Every family knew very well that when the "Goodbyes" were said, it might well be for the last time.

To move West meant many hardships and took stout hearts. It took people who were willing to brave many unknown dangers and to bear many disappointments; ones who were willing to sacrifice the comforts of home and friends to take a chance on getting something better than they had ever known.

John sold off or gave away all the household goods that were not absolutely necessary. Nothing but bare necessities were to be loaded onto the heavy wagons. Groceries and bedding were the most important. After these were loaded there was not much room for the pieces of furniture that the wives felt they "just couldn't get along without," which were often discarded as superficial weight long before the journey's end. For after they had reached rough traveling, it was all the horses could do to pull the wagons loaded with the groceries, necessary clothing and many other things that were considered absolutely indispensable. The most important thing of all was to see that the family was kept well and healthy.

After the excitement and troubles of getting started were over and they had settled down to steady traveling, Mandy and the children began to look around and enjoy the ever-changing scenery. Theirs was a long train of wagons and the wagon boss happened to be a very particular friend of John's. It was quite a jolly group of men, women and children. The children were especially too busy enjoying themselves to allow any troubles or worries to interfere with their fun. There were beautiful flowers since it was springtime and they were blooming everywhere making the wide-open prairies very lovely and they often tempted the children to venture too far causing the older folks to watch them constantly. The wagon boss was a jolly good-natured fellow who seemed to be everywhere at once: giving orders, joking and keeping everybody orderly and happy. The wagons were always kept in line; all ready for immediate action. At the first sign of Indians the wagons were always hurried into position which meant they must be placed in a circle with the horses turned towards the center of the ring. In this way, the women and children had some protection and the men could use the wagons as a sort of fortress. This was always done no matter where or when they stopped for any length of time. In this way, they were always prepared for any surprise attack. If they were fortunate in knowing just what to do and how to work together, it was to their best advantage.

Bill Bailey, the wagon boss on this particular train, was a very capable manager. It did not take the drivers long to learn the rules. Being good-natured and full of fun, he was always springing some joke on those he came in contact with, usually giving pleasure to those who participated in it.

But on one occasion his joking led to what almost resulted in tragedy for the whole train and led to fearful consequences. The wagon train had camped for the night. It was early in the morning. The sun was just beginning to peep over the distant horizon. The air was cool and crisp with a promise of warmer weather. Women were busy cooking breakfast while the men caught the horses and harnessed them. In a few moments, the men and children were all ready for breakfast, having washed their faces in cold water and dried them on rough homespun towels. The delicious breakfast consisted of bacon fried to a crisp, bannocks, and coffee with milk for the children. They were all hungry for there was nothing like outdoor air to stimulate the appetite.

Bill, the train boss, was in an extra jovial mood that morning and for good reason. They had traveled many days now with no trouble of any kind to disturb their peaceful journey. He knew that they were just now entering the Indian country. He had spent much of his life amongst the Indians and had never yet seen one that he was afraid of. He had been fortunate in never having been in any serious encounters with any of them. Usually he got along with the Indians better than most white people did, being better acquainted with the Indians and their ways.

As they were preparing to break camp, Lizzie, John's eldest daughter, was very busy folding and packing away the blankets, doing whatever was found to be done.

"Say John," Bill suddenly exclaimed, nodding toward the girls. He drew out his handkerchief to wipe away perspiration from his forehead. "You'll have to watch out for Lizzy over there with that mop of red hair. Some young Indian will be running away with her."

The young girl who had become a very pretty young lady in a surprisingly short time, as girls do have a habit of doing, blushed furiously. She knew well enough that her hair was fiery red but her bathroom mirror told her every day that it was beautiful so Bill's teasing never bothered her a bit.

"Don't worry," John answered laughingly, "With that red hair she is plenty capable of taking care of herself. I pity the Indian, whether young or old, who ever tries to lay a hand on her."

"She sure has spunk all right and that's what I like. I wouldn't mind if I were a few years younger. You would have one less girl to worry about."

At this, Lizzie laughed merrily. "Why Uncle Bill," she cried. "You are not a bit old and you know it. You are just right. One thing is for sure, one would never need to be afraid of Indians as long as you are near, unless it be because you're too reckless around them."

"You don't need to worry," Bill answered. "Maybe the reason I'm not afraid of them is that I've never been hurt by them. It's not that I've never been in danger but I'm just plain lucky. I've thought a few times that I was pretty close to the dividing line on account of them but somehow I've always managed to escape without a scratch. Even at that I have some pretty good friends among the Indians. Some of the holiest people in the world live in the West and wear feathers in their hair."

"Really," Lizzy exclaimed in surprise." I thought all Indians were wild and always on the war path."

"Oh no," Bill hastened to reply. "They are not all wild. Many of them are real friendly and have no desire to fight. In fact, they have as much fear and loathing for war as we do. Some of them only need the education that the white people have to make them good and useful citizens. One of these days they are going to get it, too. One thing is sure, if you do an Indian a favor, he will never forget it and some day he will return it in one way or another but, on the other hand, if you do him an injury, he will not forget that either and he will repay you in a way that you'll never forget."

"Well," Lizzy replied, I wish I could do them all a good turn. I would like to be on the good side of every Indian. Then I wouldn't be afraid of them. I've seen very few of them and know nothing at all that is good about them. All I know about them just scares the wits out of me whenever I think of them."

As she spoke, the girl began climbing up onto the high wagon seat with Bill helping her. "It really does no good to be afraid of them," he was saying thoughtfully. "I've always managed to get along with them fairly well and I really don't know why either, unless," with a twinkle in his eyes, "it's because I'm so good-looking."

At this they both laughed for Bill was noted for his extreme lack of beauty. "I think it is because you are so good-natured," Lizzy answered fondly. I don't see how anyone could have any trouble with you."

"Well," Bill replied, as he pinched her rosy cheeks. "I don't think you will have anything to worry about because I'm not expecting any trouble. I haven't heard of any Indians being on the warpath. Maybe they have decided that it's no fun trying to lick people who don't want to fight any worse than we do."

In the meantime, Bill had been watching a speck in the distance which was growing larger and larger as he tried to keep his little friend occupied. He surmised that it was a band of Indians and hated to see the frightened look chase away the happy smile on her face.

Suddenly she saw it, "LOOK!" She screamed. "Oh! Look! Indians!! Coming right toward us! Oh, what shall we do?"

Bill placed his cool hand on her trembling shoulder and smiled reassuringly, "Don't worry your pretty little head one bit. Just watch. Your Uncle Bill will have a little fun with them. Then you can see for yourself that they are just as jolly as white people."

In a few moments, the Indians rode up beside

them. One of them, who seemed to be the spokesman, was riding a fine big black horse. He appeared to be friendly, but there seemed something about him that struck terror to the hearts of all who were watching him just as though their eyes were glued to him.

It was just as Bill had said. He did not fear these people. He was not boasting when he said he had never had any serious trouble with them, although it would have been much better if he had been less bold and more careful, knowing full well that many of the Indians were hunting for trouble. He had always figured that the white people were to blame for most of their trouble, bringing most of it on themselves by invading the West in the first place. It was not enough that they had taken possession of the Eastern States but now they were taking over the West as well, leaving the Indians very little choice but to fight. If the whites drove them too far the Indians would fight to keep the white man from taking all they possessed.

Bill knew how the Indians felt about their white neighbors and sympathized with them while still being loyal to his own people. He had friends everywhere he went. "How!" he greeted as the Indians rode up beside the wagon.

"Ugh," The Indian answered gruffly.

"Nice horse you have there," Bill continued looking closely at the black horse.

The Indian glanced up expectantly while a crafty grin swept over his face. "You like?" he asked hopefully. He had never been known to turn away a prospective trader without first finding out how much could be gained by trading.

"Yes," Bill answered in mock seriousness, a dangerous twinkle in his eye. "You trade?"

The Indian grinned broadly, "Maybe," looking over the wagon and horses with an appraising eye. Then he caught sight of Lizzie and his face lit up with a hideous grin. Bill unfortunately remembered that the Indians were very fond of red hair. The Indian said in a business-like way as he nodded towards the frightened girl, "Trade you!" Right before the horrified gaze of all the white men he instantly dismounted and, with his black eyes on the girl, began tying his horse to the wagon wheel.

Bill gasped and his face turned a deathly white as the horrible truth dawned on him. The Indian had fooled him; had taken him at his word and intended to carry away his little friend. This probably would have happened anyway for these Indian men had no pity or sympathy for any white people.

Lizzy screamed and hid her face in her hands, almost fainting with fright. Her mother caught her in her arms. Jerking back the bedding, she hastily thrust Lizzy under it and pulled the cover over her so tightly that she almost smothered.

"I was only joking! I'm sorry!" Bill apologized as he

untied the rope from the wagon wheel and handed
it back to the scowling Indian. The man gave him
one black soul searing look and turning, bounded
nimbly onto the shiny back of his horse.

"You lie," he shouted angrily as he rode swiftly
away leaving the fear stricken people to watch as
he disappeared in a cloud of dust.

That night, not many miles away, a war dance was
taking place. Those who were participating were
not fooling themselves into thinking it was a dance
for pleasure. They had never danced with more
seriousness in their lives. There was always more
or less pleasure derived from the excitement they
always created at such times. Some wore
magnificent war bonnets made of buckskin and
trimmed with feathers of many colors sewed onto
strips of buckskin that hung down their backs.
Others merely wore a small bunch of feathers on
the tops of their heads. All wore bead belts, any
sort of bright or shiny trimming to their costumes,
with a breech cloth worn as trousers. There were
highly trimmed moccasins and plenty of paint of
many colors and designs, most of them too hideous
to imagine by any general make-up of dance
costumes.

Camp fires were burning brightly. With leaps and
bounds and much gesturing, the braves danced
wildly around: twisting, gyrating and keeping up a
constant sing song, sometimes mournful with an
occasional wild war whoop which would reverberate
through the tall trees. Drums, made of hollow trees

with hides stretched over the opening, resounded with a steady rhythmic rumble to which the nimble feet of the dancers kept surprisingly perfect time. One big Indian, grotesquely painted and not beautiful by any means, who would be capable of frightening a white child into hysterics, grinned evilly and pointed his bow and arrow in anticipation of the great battle to be fought. His eyes gleamed wickedly, his mouth set in hard lines as he threw up his arms and shot an arrow straight into the body of a night owl that had ventured too near. It fell at his feet. The Indian picked it up shouting exultingly as he tossed it up in the air and put another arrow into it before it struck the ground.

A war dance did not always mean that a war was pending; sometimes it was just for pleasure, but tonight there were no such thoughts in the mind of the Indian who had just returned from scouting around on his black horse, his heart full of anger. It was seldom that a white man could get the best of him but today he had been tricked. One had backed out on a trade and had given his comrades a chance to laugh at him. This was one more big black mark against the white people. Really, he had hated the idea of parting with his horse, especially when a white man wanted him, and the idea that he would tolerate a white woman around was ridiculous, but he could have traded her for many ponies, for red headed girls were considered quite popular with some of the Indians. Those were the kind of Indians he did not mind cheating. To make matters worse, some white traders had been there that day and had brought the Indians some fire water. He had often warned the Indians about letting the white people cheat them in their trading but the traders were wise to the weakness of the Indians and had supplied them with enough fire water to make it quite a profitable day for themselves. This was much to the disgust of the Indian leader who had completely lost control of the Indians after they had drunk the stuff the traders had left them.

He did not drink himself. With some of the other men to help him, he tried to keep some order and to keep anyone from getting hurt. He found that it was useless to try, for his drink crazed friends had gone completely wild.

Seeing that he could do nothing with them, he joined in the dance where he soon became so interested in relieving his feelings which were seething inside him over the traders and other hateful fire water that he left the drinking savages to themselves for a while. Seeing his brother-in-law Eagle Eye, who was now quite drunk, sitting beside the fire, he went in and sat down beside him. He had heard him grumble a little earlier in the evening and knew that his wayward brother was very angry about something. This was bad, very bad as almost anything could happen at such a time. He was worried as he sat there undecided as to what he should do. Finally, he threw his long arms across the drooping shoulders of the angry brave. "What's the trouble brother?" he asked anxiously. Then his voice grew stern, as he saw how completely the liquor had overpowered his brother. "Why do you drink the fire water the white men bring here? It is no good. It is bad for you. Why do you try to be like the white people anyway? You trade with him and he gives you fire water. Then he cheats you. He comes here to get all you have and then he says he is here to teach us his ways. For what he teaches us, a few trinkets, beads and bright colored calico, we give the best things we have; our horses, our living, everything! The more fire water he can get us to drink the more he can cheat us. The fire water makes demons out of good Indians. Someday there'll be no Indians. Someday this beautiful country will be all theirs. Our homes will be gone and we will have no place to live except where they tell us. We will not be free anymore. The white people will tell us what we can and cannot do. Then it will be the white man's turn to give and, as always, he will give us as little as possible. Why do you drink his fire water? Why do you get drunk and let him cheat you all the time?"

Eagle Eye looked at his brother with blood shot eyes. What was his favorite brother talking about anyway? He was so angry with the white people but not just now at any rate. He was having a good time except that he was still very angry with someone back there in the crowd. Who was it? Try as he might he could not remember who it was or what he was angry about. But the words "fire water" touched a vibrant chord in his otherwise drink deadened brain and he rose slowly to his feet. "Fire water," was all he said. "Fire water! That's why." Then he staggered away with a backward glance. His friend watched him as he disappeared among the dancers. There was anger in his heart; great anger, but there was pity in his eyes. He got up and joined the dancers once more. The anger in his heart seemed to lend wings to his feet. For a while he danced like mad. As he saw how the fire water was affecting his people, his anger grew until as the morning drew near he was ready for almost anything. Then came the climax to his night of anguish. Some of the warriors came to him carrying Eagle Eye. One glance proved to him that his worst fears were correct. His brother was dead. He had been killed in a drunken fight. After a hasty examination, he hung his head in grief, "thus was the end."

Eagle Eye, son of their chief, was dead and his death was caused by the drinking of the white man's fire water. A loud wail rent the air as the full realization of the terrible tragedy struck home in the hearts of the people. Suddenly he sprang to his feet, his dark eyes blazing dangerously. "Come," he shouted, "We have danced all night and, because of the white man's fire water, death has visited us! Come! We must have revenge!"

So, while it was still dark, for there was no moon to give the morning darkness a little light, and while the sad wail was sounding throughout the Indian village, a silent army of painted savages wended its way through the trees and out onto the prairies. Very quietly he raised his hands and cupped them to his mouth. "Whoooo," sounded through the early dawn.

"Was it a wolf?" someone may have asked.
"Whoooo," came a reply from over the prairie -
"Whoooo," came from another direction. Then he
nodded his head, a satisfied grin spreading over his
dark face.

CHAPTER IX   Indians

[3]Crossing the plains about three day's drive behind our friends the Wynecoops was another train. It was not such a long train for these people had not taken the time that would have been necessary to have gotten up such a large group of people, a mistake that many of the pioneers did not live to tell about.

A man and woman sat on the front seat of one of the wagons. The man's name was Amos Wells. He wore a wide black hat from under which a pair of sharp blue eyes peered. His good-natured face was almost covered with a thick red beard. His wife was a small dark eyed woman wearing a blue sunbonnet. She wore a long blue homespun dress which was much the worse for wear, although clean and neatly patched.

Between them sat a beautiful young girl with bright golden curls. She was about 18 years old and had her mother's lovely features but her large eyes were as blue as the sky above. She also was wearing a sunbonnet and her pink dress reached to her slim ankles, long wide skirts being the height of fashion at that time for both elderly women and young alike. She was laughing and talking gaily as they rode along. There was much to interest her on this, her first trip across the plains.

---

[3] (c.1861)

In the wagon under the canvas were several small children who were romping and playing together. This steady traveling day by day was beginning to get tiresome to them. Sometimes they would get out and run along beside the wagons gathering flowers but they would soon become tired of that and would climb back into the wagon.

Della, the oldest girl, always rode up on the front seat with her parents. She loved to watch the many changes of the beautiful scenery and to spend her time gazing out over the wild stretches of prairie land or at the distant hills in admiration intermixed with a little fear of the unknown.

One day, to her great delight, she made the discovery that a wagon train was just ahead of them. Instantly the hope of a chance to lengthen out their wagon train and thus secure better protection flashed through the young girl's mind. There was the thrill that only a young person knows of meeting people you have never seen before.

Oh Daddy," she cried greatly excited, "there's a wagon train ahead of us. See right ahead there! Look! Wagon tracks just ahead of us! Hurry, let's catch up with them." She became so excited that she jumped down off the wagon seat and began running alongside the wagon shouting the news to those further back who could not see the tracks. Suddenly, she stopped dead in her tracks, turned and ran towards their own wagon. Her face which had been sparkling a moment before was now deathly white, for there, a short distance away, sitting astride their ponies were three Indians watching her intently.

They had seen Indians several times before but they had all been friendly and had not caused them much uneasiness, but these Indians did not seem inclined to be friendly. They merely sat on their ponies while they appeared to be trying to decide among themselves and at the same time size up the wagon train. Suddenly they wheeled their horses around and rode away, soon disappearing from sight.

Oh, Daddy!" Della cried as she hastily climbed up beside her father. "Now we must hurry and catch up with that train ahead of us. I'm terribly afraid. Those men acted so strangely. Did you notice how they kept watching me? Oh Daddy - Daddy, please hurry. We must catch up with those people ahead of us because I know those awful Indians are coming back."

Just then the wagon boss rolled up with a worried look on his tanned face. He drew his horse up beside Amos' wagon. "Say," he exclaimed anxiously. "Did you notice how hostile those Indians acted, especially the one on the big black horse? I've seen lots of Indians in my time and I've always noticed that whenever they stand back the way those fellows did, then ride away without showing any signs of being friendly, they always come back - only there will be more of them."

Amos glanced up in quick alarm. "Yes, I did notice their peculiar actions," he answered guardedly, not wanting Della to hear them. "Della says they were watching her a lot. She is very worried about it and wants us to hurry and catch up with the wagon train ahead of us. Think we can make it?"

The experienced wagon boss shook his head, "No use," he said. "It won't hurt anything to try. We can at least do the best we can. This little wagon train wouldn't stand a chance against a band of red skins who were really on the war path. To tell the truth, I am afraid that is exactly what we are in for. I don't think there's one chance in a million of catching that train ahead though because, for some reason, they seem to be in an awful hurry themselves. I know we are not very far behind them and still we haven't even gotten a glimpse of them so far."

In a few minutes, every driver was urging his team along as fast as he could make them go. In every wagon, guns were being loaded and prepared for instant use. Women bowed their heads in prayer while little children knelt beside them. Fear gripped every heart and drained the blood from every stricken face. At a distance a dark cloud became visible. Nearer and nearer it came. Soon it was near enough to be recognized as a cloud of dust which meant only one thing - Indians!! Now becoming very frightened, the women began throwing away everything that could possibly make the load lighter for the horses to pull. The men were throwing all their energy into making the horses do their best. The poor beasts were urged to go faster and faster until they fairly flew over the rough ground. The children clung to the sideboards of the wagon or anything that would give them support for fear of being thrown out in their mad haste to escape from the evil that was slowly but surely overtaking them.

But the men knew their efforts were to no avail. The Indians were gaining on them and there was no doubt as to their intentions. Some of the children began to show their fear with wails and tears. The women tried to comfort them while their own hearts were quaking with the great fear that only parents with children who are in fearful danger of meeting a horrible death can realize.

The wagon boss gave swift orders and almost immediately every driver had turned his team. Without a moment's hesitation, commotion or a moment of precious time wasted, every wagon was in its place and every man had his gun ready. There was a sob on every lip and a prayer in every heart.

On the yelling savages came! The dark faces outlined in the thick dust, fierce and evil looking, could now be seen. Suddenly the air rang with the Indian's horrible war cry: a cry that once heard was never forgotten. The Indians began circling the wagon train which was now formed into a make shift stockade behind which children and women loaded guns for their valiant men folks.

Around and around the yelling mob circled, their

ponies stretched out with long tails streaming in the wind. The wide circle grew smaller and smaller while the brave men in the wagon train waited, guns loaded, aimed and ready. Galloping in steady motion, yelling and screeching madly, with brown naked bodies glistening in the sun, the Indians swayed on the backs of their many-colored ponies.

Finally, they were within shooting distance. Simultaneously every man fired. Bang! Bang! The shots rang out and many of the red skins fell to the ground. This did not halt the other Indians for an instant.

Onward they came, arrows flying from their bows in answer to the steady roar of the guns fired from under the wagons. Many of the Indians fell from their frantic ponies never to rise again, but the circling screaming mob never faltered. In the poor shelter of the wagon train, whenever a man dropped his gun and lay still, some woman with a sob in her heart would pick it up and take her husband's place; perhaps her place soon to be taken by a small son or daughter.

Still the savages came on, nearer and nearer, until they were within the little fortress, fighting hand to hand; fighting desperately, horribly, for life is very dear and hard to give up.

Suddenly a huge painted Indian grabbed Della around the waist holding her tightly, sprang onto a big black horse and started to ride off with her. The white people were fighting a losing battle and they knew it. When they saw the struggling frightened girl grasped in the arms of the red man they knew nothing in the world could save her now. Bang! A single shot rang out. Merciful death claimed her, saving her from a fate many times more horrible. Bang! Once more a shot rang out but this time the aim was not so good. The Indian letting the body of the girl slide to the ground, whirled and sent an arrow flying straight to the mark, for he never missed. He had lost again but they had been revenged.

Amos looked around him. His wife and children were all dead. A horse stood in a clump of trees nearby. Cautiously crawling on his stomach under the wagons, Amos managed to get among some rocks. In all the smoke and dust the Indians had not noticed him. Crawling from rock to rock he finally managed to reach the trees. Then, dodging from tree to tree, he reached the horse without being discovered. Amos sprang onto the horse's back, swiftly turned him around and made a dash for freedom, not a moment too soon, for some of the Indians had seen him and a shower of arrows struck him and his horse. Since none of the arrows were very deep because of the long distance they were shot from, the horse only ran the faster. Amos knew that he was running a race with death. The only chance he had to save his friends was to get help. Their ammunition was almost gone so help would have to come soon. He dropped behind the horse as the horse ran and hung there. Finally, the arrows stopped flying; the Indians, evidently thinking they had killed him, did not waste any

more of their arrows on him. All that saved him
was the Indians being too busy to go after his scalp.
But the plucky horse kept running even after they
were well out of shooting range. Just as Amos was
beginning to think that he was practically safe and
would perhaps still be able to get help for his
friends, he heard the terrible victory cry of the red
skins. He knew that it was now too late. He glanced
back and saw a great cloud of smoke reaching
towards the sky and knew that the Indians had
just ended another terrible massacre by burning
the wagon train. Amos bowed his head in grief
while burning tears rolled down his weather-beaten
cheeks. He soon found the tracks of the train ahead
and followed them as fast as he could make his
poor horse travel. He was afraid every moment that
the Indians would see him and kill him before he
could get to the people ahead. He knew where he
could find comparative safety for himself from the
howling mob but it was not his safety he was
thinking of. He knew that if they saw him they
would soon find the wagon tracks he was following.

On and on the horse galloped. Terror seemed to
lend wings to his feet. Amos could no longer see or
hear the Indians but this did not lessen his fear in
the least. He knew how easy it would be for them to
follow him if they still wanted to find him. The
wagon train ahead had left deep tracks in the soft
soil.

In one of the wagons ahead a baby girl had died
leaving great sorrow in every wagon. She had been
a sweet child and they all loved her very dearly.

She had not been strong and traveling in the heavy lumbering wagon over rocks and deeply rutted trails had proved too much for her delicate health. She had passed away during one of the long harassing nights while they were trying so hard to put as much distance as possible between themselves and the Indians.

They were all tired and hungry for the fear of the Indians had prevented them from making fires or stopping in any place longer than was absolutely necessary. They had traveled night and day since meeting the Indians, only stopping long enough to snatch a few bites of food and to feed and water their stock whenever they became too jaded to travel to any advantage.

That morning they had halted long enough to give the horses a short rest. Since then, they had been pushing steadily, halting only for a few moments whenever the horses were too winded to go on without a little rest.

During the day, they had crossed a wide stream of water and while the horses were wading through, they had drunk their fill. This had been a wonderful help. To find plenty of water while crossing the plains was always a great blessing to travelers at any time and especially to those who were so unfortunate as to be fleeing from Indians or other danger.

But now, late in the afternoon, Bill knew that the best they could do to show their love for their little friend was to stop and give the baby a decent burial. Bill, with whom the little girl had been a great favorite, gave orders that they halt a short time and have the funeral. Soon another little grave marked the trail of the pioneers. After the simple funeral, they moved on. The thought of leaving the little grave alone away out on the plains was heartbreaking to them but there was no other way.

They went a few miles on down the trail where they decided to stop and rest for an hour or so to give their horses a chance to eat and rest, too, especially since there had been no sign of the Indians. They were beginning to have hopes that so much haste might be unnecessary for now.

They had eaten a cold lunch as they were still very uneasy about building fires. The men and women were busy doing the small chores which riding over the rough roads made it impossible to do at other times. The children were taking advantage of the opportunity to relax and exercise their muscles by running around and around the wagons doing all the lively stunts that children seem to delight in doing.

But Lizzie anxiously watched the distant horizon, having been uneasy all day for she could not forget the look on the face of the Indian on the black horse as he had ridden away. She felt certain that he meant to return. Bill heartily regretted the careless words he had spoken to the Indian since it had caused the girl so much anxiety. He apologized for his rashness. He was becoming very confident that the Indians would not follow them after such a lapse of time. In fact, he had been certain of this for some time but, out of consideration for the others, he had kept his opinions to himself.

Suddenly Lizzy sprang to her feet, horror written all over her face, as she pointed down the trail they had just been traveling.

"There they come now!" she screamed, as she staggered towards the wagon. Every face turned deadly white. Coming towards them on a dead run was a lone horse and rider.

As he drew nearer they could see that it was a white man and he was covered with blood from his head to his heels. The rider failed to see arrows protruding from the bleeding, lather covered flanks of his faithful horse. As he drew near the man swayed drunkenly on the back of his horse, then slid off onto the ground before anyone could catch him.

"Indians!" He gasped as he raised himself up on his elbow. He was weak from loss of blood resulting from the wounds he had received but had scarcely noticed during the conflict. The wounds had kept bleeding profusely during those many hours of hard riding.

"Indians! Hundreds of them! HURRY, hurry! Get your wagons ready and move on! Don't stop for anything."

Instantly every man turned towards the horses and every woman and child hurried to gather up their camping outfits and pile them back into the wagons, climbing in themselves.

In less time than it takes to tell, they had the poor man, who turned out to be Amos, into one of the wagons. The suffering horse was quietly put out of his misery and they were ready to move on.

Scarcely a word was spoken as they passed on down the trail. Every eye was searching the horizon. Every face was set and white. Every heart was filled with the terrible fear that nothing in the world could equal: the fear of a horrible death by Indians. They traveled all night long, uphill and down, over roads that were scarcely good cow trails. Roads that led down into deep gulches with scarcely a track wide enough to get the wagons through, sometimes so narrow that it was with great difficulty they were able to keep their wagons on four wheels. Crossing streams in the dark was the most dangerous part of the journey but drowning was much to be preferred to being massacred by the Indians so they continued to push on.

Sometimes the horses became so exhausted that there was nothing to do but to stop a few minutes and let them rest and eat a few bites. To Lizzy, these moments were filled with sheer torture. She loved horses very dearly but nothing mattered now but to get out of this terrible Indian infested country as soon as possible.

Bill knew enough about the Indians to know they would not strike before morning. Thus, the further they could travel while covered with the darkness of the night, the better their chances were of escaping the Indians.

So, all night the children, worn out with the jolting of the heavy wagons, slept. The younger ones slept soundly. Those old enough to have a full realization of the dangers that were stalking them slept restlessly, the cold hand of fear waking them in terror at every unusual sound. The men desperately urged the horses to move faster and faster, while the weary-eyed women anxiously kept watch over all, listening intently for any strange sound that may be a warning to them. They were straining their eyes in the darkness for fear the treacherous enemy might sneak up on them, catch them unawares and murder the whole train without giving them a chance to defend themselves.

Just before the break of day, Bill called a halt to feed their jaded horses. This was absolutely necessary for it would be foolhardy to go on until the poor animals dropped in their tracks. Bill knew that if they must stop and rest, it was much safer to do so now before daylight.

They had been resting for a short time, long enough for the horses to finish their feed of oats. The men had not unhitched them and had merely hung their nose bags in place, when suddenly there came the sound of a lone coyote, a long lonesome wail which filled the air and was immediately answered by another cry farther away.

The sound coming so suddenly in the darkness which seemed thick enough to cut with a knife, filled all their hearts with greater fear and startled all into immediate action.

"Say, Bill," John whispered anxiously as Bill came hurriedly up to the Wynecoop wagon. "I didn't like the sound of that coyote howling. What did you make of it? Did it sound natural to you?"

"Oh, yes. Those were coyotes alright. No doubt about it! But let's get going! Even if they were only coyotes, they make me nervous just the same. You never can tell whether it's a four-legged one or one with two legs. Anyway, I'm for reaching a favorite spot myself before we do any more camping."

"That's my sentiments exactly," John heartily replied as he hurriedly pulled the nose bags from the heads of his horses and climbed back onto the wagon seat.

As quietly as possible the long wagon train started out another day of torturous fleeing from danger. Constant watchfulness and awful suspense was the vigil. When morning dawned, there was no sign of Indians. This was a great relief but Bill knew that those coyotes yelping may very well have been Indians calling to each other. Such things have been known to happen and it could happen again.

Bill urged every driver to do his best. This was all
that was necessary to almost cause a panic. Once
more they put every effort in making their horses
travel faster and faster. The clumsy wagons were
rolling, swaying and jumping over the road like
something alive fleeing ahead of a prairie fire. They
turned the corners without slowing causing wagons
with their high canvas covers to careen crazily,
sometimes almost tipping over, never slackening
their pace except to slow up on the hills or to cross
a stream.

Night came once more. Bill decided that the horses
could not possibly go on any longer without food
and rest. They made camp for the night. They were
too tired to keep awake, almost too tired to care
anymore whether the Indians caught up with them
or not. They were too tired to even think straight
any longer. They were completely worn out.

The men took turns watching all during the long
dreary night but not a sound came to disturb the
stillness. All was peaceful and quiet. The worn-out
horses grazed and rested until dawn.

With early dawn, reassurance came that there was
still no sign of Indians and the wagon train knew
they were close to friendly territory. What a relief!
The women knelt down and thanked God for their
deliverance while tears streamed down the faces of
the hardened men and were stealthily wiped away.
They all wept in sorrow for the people who had
been in the train behind them, who they felt had

given their lives in ransom for theirs. The tears
helped to wipe away some of the bitterness of the
horrible nightmare they had just passed through.

Amos had told them of all that had happened and
especially about Della, the beautiful girl with the
golden hair. When they were finally convinced that
they were no longer being pursued by the red skins,
Bill had made up his mind that he alone had been
to blame for it all. He knew that his little joke on
his dearest friend had led to the terrible tragedy.

"Amos," he said brokenly, "you take my place. You
are well enough now to ride a horse. You take my
horse and lead these people to California. I'm not
fit to be a wagon boss or any other kind of boss.
But," he continued, "I never thought that an Indian
would get angry at a joke. I've joked with them
many a time but this is the first time I ever had
any trouble over one. I've had a lot of fun with
them, but I guess this goes to prove that they are
like other people in some ways. Some will take a
joke and others will resent them, especially if it is
on them."

But what Bill did not know was that, at the very
moment that he was wondering about the Indian
who would not laugh with him, the Indian was
exultantly laughing at him. His revenge was
complete and he knew it, or thought he did.

"Oh, well," Amos replied as he stooped to pick up a
stick and began whittling on it. "I think those
fellows were hunting trouble and it didn't take

much to start it. They sort of came with a chip on their shoulders and you were the one who accidentally knocked it off."

"That may be," Bill answered, "but I still wish you would take this job. I'm such a blundering old fool that I'm not safe. That was a crazy thing for me to do and you know it as well as I do."

"No, I don't know anything of the kind," Amos replied kindly. "I do know how you feel about it and I'll be glad to help you any way I can but I honestly think it was coming before you even spoke to that fellow."

"What makes you think that?" Bill asked hopefully.

"Because," Amos answered thoughtfully, "I know human nature well enough to know that it takes very little to start a fight with anyone who is out looking for one. I think those fellows were out on the warpath and God knows why our train happened to fall into their clutches instead of yours."

"I hope you are right," Bill replied in a relieved tone. "I know that was a crazy thing for me to do but I honestly hope that I didn't cause the death of all those good people with my blundering tongue."

"No! I'm sure you didn't" Amos said, as he placed his hand affectionately on his new friend's shoulder. "Now let's talk about something else. In the first place, I would make a poor wagon boss because I don't even know the country. We would be lost inside of twenty-four hours if I was their leader. These people are your responsibility and they all depend on you not me. Don't fail them now after all they have been through."

"I guess you are right," Bill exclaimed with quick understanding. "I guess you are really right." Then, turning quickly he began preparations for another day. "We'll reach California or bust! After we get there we'll do our part towards making the Golden West the best place in the world."

So, the covered wagon crept steadily along day after day, each day bringing its own change of scenery or mode of travel. No matter how well they might be getting along, they always had small streams and wide rivers to contend with. They never knew exactly what to expect. Sometimes what was usually a small stream or creek had become a raging torrent either because of melting snow in the mountains or a heavy rain storm. In either case, they were compelled to build a raft.

If the stream was not too deep they could ford it but otherwise they used a raft which was built of logs and tied together with heavy wire or ropes. If they had a few boards and some heavy nails they could nail it together. It all depended on what material they might have with them.

After the goods were all piled on the raft along with the women and children, they were ready to go. If there happened to be anything left from their wild race with the Indians that was too heavy or too clumsy to take on the raft, there was nothing to do but leave it behind. In that way, Mandy was obliged to give up a much-prized dresser over which she could not keep from shedding a few tears.

Crossing these rivers was often very dangerous. They were sometimes very deep and treacherous, making the crossing of them on rafts quite exciting to say the least. Occasionally a load would be washed away and go floating down the river. This was hard on the man who lost it, for it could very easily be all he owned in the world. The horses and cattle were made to swim across and it was seldom that any of them were lost.

At times, they would cross miles and miles of prairie land spreading in every direction, covered with heavy bunch grass, dotted here and there with beautiful wild flowers. Then would come the heavy timber and hills. Whenever there were hills there would be deep gullies and generally more streams of water. Of course, there were no real bridges and the roads were mere trails, sometimes not even that, but just signs along the way that sometime or other people had travelled that way.

One morning they awoke and were very much surprised to see a large herd of buffalo grazing quietly some distance away. Some of the men were determined to take their guns after some fresh meat. Bill refused to allow it. "No boys," he said, "I'm sorry but we absolutely can't afford to take chances. There may be Indians trailing the buffalo, and you know as well as I do what that would mean."

"Oh, shucks," one of the men grumbled. "Who's afraid? If there were any Indians around those animals wouldn't be standing there grazing. There's not an Indian around. Besides those buffalo are standing so still we could be right onto them before they saw us. Bang! Bang! Bang! and we'd have enough meat to last us until we reached California. I'm going and nobody is going to stop me!" Then he grabbed his gun and started to jump onto a horse that was standing nearby.

"No, you are not going, " Bill answered steadily. "You are going to stay right here. I've had enough trouble with those fellows. We may need meat alright but we have no lives to spare for it."

"I guess you're right Bill," the young would-be hunter murmured as he walked back to his wagon. Suddenly he stopped dead still as he pointed excitedly towards the herd that had become frightened and was now galloping across the prairie, a regular thundering stampede. "Yes, I know you are right Bill. Look! Indians! I can almost feel my skull coming loose already." Bill grinned but his face was white as he turned towards the others. "I reckon we'd better be moving along," he said very quietly, "but make as little noise as possible. Being in this ravine may help us to keep out of the Indian's sight if we are careful.

"Thank God they are headed the other way,"
someone whispered as he prepared to start. "Yes,
and thank God for Bill too while you're at it," came
from the young fellow who wanted to go hunting.
"If it hadn't been for him, those red skins would be
chasing us instead of buffalo right now."

The experience they had with the Indians had
proved to them that they could not be too careful.
In a very short time they were moving stealthily to
safer territory. They travelled all that day without
seeing any more of the Indians. That night they felt
that it would be safe to camp. They decided that it
would not be so dangerous traveling from then on
and that the Indians they had seen were not on the
war path at all but were just hunting and minding
their own business.

From there they traveled all together for a few days
longer until they finally came to the parting of the
ways. Some of the train went up into the Oregon
country, while John Wynecoop and some of the
others continued on to California, the Golden State.

Of course, the real gold rush days were practically
over, the days of '49, but everywhere people were
taking up homesteads along the Sacramento Valley
and here John decided to settle. He chose a place
near Marysville where he felt he could be happy
and where he thought in time, he could build a
lovely home. But how many of us know just what
the future holds for us? Although we make all our
plans and they seem perfect us, how many of us
have had all our dreams come true?

CHAPTER X   Medicine Man

In the meantime, Fred finally decided to settle in
Marcus. This was a small town on the banks of the
Columbia River. He heard that there was plenty of
fighting in the other states, but the Indians around
Marcus were more peaceful. Further east the Civil
War was still raging and he often wondered how
his mother and three brothers were faring. He
wondered if they were all still alive and if his
sisters were married yet. He seldom heard from
them anymore since the war had started for it was
hard to make connections, the country so divided
and torn up in conflict. Those of his brothers who
were large slaveholders, now fighting to save their
property, would probably be having plenty of
trouble. He never ceased to hope that the Yankees
would win the war for this being the land of the
free. He thought that all people, regardless of color,
should have an equal chance to live in freedom.
Color did not figure in his way of reasoning. His
skin was white as a Negro was black and an Indian
was red. That was all there was to it. Each
nationality had its own way of living, thinking and
working, but they were all human and should have
equal rights in this beautiful land of America.

He was glad that he was far away from the strain
and upheavals of the Civil War. He had traveled far
to get to where he could work in his own profession,
healing the sick and helping those who needed
help. It was hard for the Indians to put the
necessary confidence in any white man and for this

they were not to blame. Most of the white people had come out West just for their own special interests and many of them were not even honest in their dealings with the Indians, thinking that they had a perfect right to anything they could get away with from the Indians, as the Indians could be cheated into accepting little for whatever the white man wanted.

Often, they would trade bright colored calico worth a few cents per yard in actual value, pretty glass beads or a small amount of tobacco for furs that the unsuspecting Indians had worked hard to get. They would sell the furs for a small fortune. Of course, not all of the Indians were so ignorant and these degradations were not passed unobserved by those who knew the value of the furs. Occasionally it was incidents such as these that led to fierce battles and the loss of many lives on both sides.

The Indians as a general rule were ignorant and superstitious which had a tendency toward making them very susceptible to the superior knowledge of things by their white neighbors. In this way, the white people soon managed to gain possession of most of the rich grazing land throughout the surrounding country in spite of the red man's brave fight to save for himself that which the Great Spirit had given him, but aside from the fact that they had managed to slaughter a great number of white people, they might as well try to remove a mountain from its natural resting place as to try to rid the country of the white people.

Wars were raging around what later became
Spokane Falls, Walla Walla and the Big Horn
countries. The Indians were beginning to realize
that they were powerless to stop the invasion of the
white people.

Small wonder that, when a white man was so
unfortunate as to fall into the eager clutches of a
band of Indians, he knew that the Indian would
take advantage of this opportunity by venting on
his defenseless body the rage and contempt they
felt for all their white faces.

Around the little town of Marcus, the Indians were
fast becoming reconciled to the idea of having these
strange people as neighbors. Being of a more
peaceable nature, these Indians had never suffered
as much from the white people as the fierce tribes
who lived farther south. Nevertheless, they were
always prepared for trouble. The white people
trusted the Indians just about as much as the
Indians trusted them. The white people were there
to make money and some cared very little how they
made it. Even though the majority may have been
honest, the unscrupulous men mingling with them
made it extremely dangerous for all concerned.

There were a number of garrisons situated in
different parts of the country. McDonald's
Blockhouse was not far from Marcus. Fort Spokane
was located where the Spokane River empties into
the Columbia River. The soldiers at these garrisons
could always be called upon to help in any
emergency which might arise at any time. Fred was

not a trader in any sense of the word but merely helped at whatever there was to do. If Fred happened to be at one of the forts, he often traveled with the men who were in the business of trading furs on their trips up north. But he had no interest in furs. He cared more for the people he met.

He was also interested in a steamboat on which he was working whenever he was near the coast where the boat was built. It was the first one that had ever gone over the rough places of the Columbia River so far north. Best of all was the fact that he had helped to build it. But no matter what kind of work he was doing, he was working continually to gain the confidence of the Indians, for without that he was useless to them in his profession. Often, he would try to help someone who was sick but, not trusting him, they would prefer their own Medicine Man. The fact that he had saved the little girl from drowning had won him many friends but had not won him the place in the hearts of the people that he had hoped for. Many of them still eyed him suspiciously whenever he offered to help them and refused to take his medicine. Calling for their own medicine men in times of sickness was a custom which caused Fred to spend many hours walking the floor of his cabin, trying to puzzle the inner mind of the Indian.

To any white man, the actions of the medicine men were nothing short of barbarous. No matter how sick the person might be: man, woman or child, the performance was always the same. The sick person would be placed on the floor with the sorrowing relatives around when suddenly there would come a familiar jingling sound causing the Indians to stand back making way for the great Medicine Man who would come like a whirlwind, jumping, gyrating and dancing.

Around and around he would dance; bells a jingling, feathers flopping from side to side, while from his mouth would issue forth the most unearthly sounds that Fred had ever heard. Then, throwing himself across the patient, he would rudely grasp him by the shoulders and shake him unmercifully, pounding him all the while, yelling wildly, growling and even biting him frenziedly. After the treatment had been administered for some time, the patient was probably dead. If not, he had become very much alive without any question.

Fred knew enough about the Indians to know that it would be very foolish for any white man to offer his services while the Indians were in this state of mind. They could find some excuse if the patient should die but there was no hope of saving the life of a white doctor should the patient have the same misfortune while under his care. If a white man valued his life at a time like this, he was wise to keep his opinion to himself. Fred had made up his mind to learn the Indian language which he had found rather difficult but not impossible. In this way, he found that he not only could understand the Indians much better, it was the surest way to earn their respect. One day Fred sat talking to an old priest who had spent many years amongst the

Indians.

Why do the medicine men paint their faces so ugly when they come to help the sick?" He asked. They frighten the poor little children half to death just to look at them. And why do they blow on the sick and go through all the other crazy maneuvers?"

"One thing sure," the priest replied. "They don't scare away the evil spirits and that is what their object is. They all lay their sickness to evil spirits and think this is the only way to get rid of them. A white doctor does nothing to frighten them away, therefore he is no good to the sick even though he may have made the patient feel much better. The relatives only think that the evil spirit is just waiting nearby to carry him away at any moment or when the doctor leaves."

"How terrible," Fred exclaimed, "I came all the way out West purposely to help these poor superstitious people but I seem to be getting nowhere fast."

One day Fred heard the dreaded word the Indians used for "Small Pox" whispered around. He immediately was greatly alarmed for he knew well the terrible consequences for a smallpox epidemic among the Indians. It would be worse than the worst war they had ever experienced. There was nothing to compare with it for it would mow them down like wheat in the fields and he knew by past experiences how powerless he would be to help them.

He learned, however, that the epidemic was not among the Colville Indians but among the Spokanes about 100 miles away. It was doing its ravaging work unchecked by anyone and the destruction wrought by the plague was horrible.

Whole families died of it. The poor people had no way of dealing with unknown disease. Such was their horror of it that the mere sight of one who had it was enough to drive hundreds of people out in all kinds of weather, panic stricken, to wildly seek refuge in the hills or anywhere away from the terrible black death. Those who had escaped direct contact with the disease tried desperately to keep from being exposed. Those who had contracted it vainly tried to escape from their own sickness, many of them dying along the way. Anyone who was unfortunate or brave enough to find them and not run away would dig a hole in the ground and roll the body into it with a long pole. Then the hole would be carefully filled with rocks and dirt.

Here the medicine men were helpless and as badly frightened as their patients, many of them dying along with the people from whom they were supposed to be driving away the evil spirits. In their fear and desperation, the Indians were becoming more willing to accept the assistance of the white doctor, but for hundreds of Indians it was too late. Fred heard of the extermination of most of the Spokane tribe and it made him feel very badly to know that he might have saved so many of them had he only known in time and been allowed to use his knowledge for their benefit. Nevertheless, it

gave him considerable satisfaction to know that he
was gaining the confidence of the Colville Indians
and, for that reason, he knew that he would be able
to help them stamp out the plague before it did so
much damage should it finally reach them. But
somehow or other, it never reached them and they
were spared the awful tragedy that had befallen
their friends and neighbors.

Marcus was only a small place but the surrounding
country was beautiful with the ever-changing
beauty of a country with many variations of
industry. The great Columbia River, with its clean
blue waters running deep and grand to look upon,
was a real source of usefulness in many ways.
Steamboats, as time went by, were a great help to
the fur trading business and fishing was a very
practical way of supplying the people with food.
The surrounding hills and rocky mountains were
covered with heavy timber and were well-stocked
with wild game. The Kettle River roared madly
through the chasm worn deep by the many years of
constant wear of the ever-hurrying water over a
steep rocky bed, rushing to join the majestic
Columbia. The hills and flats along the river banks
were covered with tall grass where cattle roamed at
will or rested fully satisfied.

Farther on down the Columbia River was Kettle
Falls. Here the mighty river appeared to have gone
wild in the commotion it made, acting as though it
had simply gone mad. Great boulders lay along the
riverbed over which the waters roared loudly,
swirling swiftly around the mountainous rocks as if

angry at their presence, leaping high in the air and falling back with a loud roar, then going on its way as if determined to reach the Pacific Coast at any cost.

Here was where the Indians went in crowds to catch their winter's supply of fish. Teepees dotted the shores with frames set up on which to dry fish that were brought in by the braves who had caught them in their fish traps and with sharp spears made of bone. Salmon were plentiful and so there was no danger of going hungry in the winter if they had plenty of dried fish. Fishing was a great sport among the Indians, besides being a valuable source of meat supply for them. During the salmon season the men were very busy, as the season did not last long, and there was much to be done. Some of the Indians used wooden spears, being made of Thornberry wood which is very hard and strong and always available along the banks of the river, but many preferred the fish traps or snares. These were made of willows which were very green and very pliable at this time of the year. They were woven together to form a deep narrow basket, closed at one end. Then a funnel shaped entrance was made and bound with small willow branches. The funnel shaped entrance was pointed towards the bottom. Once in the traps or snares it was impossible for a salmon to escape for he could never find his way to the small end of the funnel. This made a very serviceable trap. As the fisherman was usually watching on a platform built over the trap it was only a matter of seconds until the big shiny fish lay flopping on the sandy shore. As the salmon were very plentiful, it was not long until the women were as busy as bees for it was their job to clean and dry them. This was done by first cutting a salmon down the front and cleaning them and then cutting them almost to the skin down each side to the backbone. The salmon were spread out flat, cutting them across side to side almost to the skin but not through it. They were held spread out with sharp sticks so they could not fold up. The prepared fish was laid on a rack made of green willows or cottonwood sticks or fastened to sticks stuck in the ground and left to dry, either before a slow fire or in the sunshine. Later they could be eaten as they were boiled or simply held before a hot fire and broiled. They were a very satisfactory addition to any meal.

Trout, squaw fish, suckers and white fish could be caught at any time of the year. Winter or summer, men and women could be seen along almost any stream fishing for whatever fish were most plentiful at that particular season of the year. Suckers were most plentiful in the spring of the year and the men who were most clever with the spear could jerk them out of the water just as fast as they could manipulate the spear to remove the fish from the hook. They were not as good as the salmon, being quite bony but they answered the purpose whenever they were needed. The Indians were very clever at separating the bones from the meat, even though the bones were very sharp and tiny. The meat was of much finer texture than the salmon and was quite satisfactory to the hungry braves and their families.

It was the man's job to furnish the meat for the family but the women had to furnish other kinds of food such as camas, a plant that grew in patches which was dug up. The small brown bulb was dried to be used that way or made into bread. Then there were the bitter roots which were dried and boiled before using. Berries of all kinds grew in abundance almost anywhere at certain times of the year. They were picked and dried by these busy women who were seldom idle and who wished for nothing more than to be left alone. They were happy in their own way and felt since their own way had carried them through so many years it could still carry them on the same way and they would be satisfied.

Many of them lived in the beautiful strip of country called the Colville Valley where the Colville River runs smoothly and peacefully through a valley alternately bordered on each side with low hills covered with green grass and trees or high steep mountains covered with timber and thick brush where huckleberries grew abundantly and wild deer roamed unafraid.

Down in the valley the cattle grazed lazily enjoying the thick green grass or lying in the shade of the heavy brush along the river bank. The Colville River was only a small stream but it was slow and lazy looking, a place where children loved to play.

Fred had traveled the world over, had visited many foreign countries, had crossed the U.S. but he knew that here was home to him. Here among the Colville Indians, the people he loved, some still viewed him with distrust. Fred knew of one white man who caused a massacre by not being able to save a patient and he knew that there was only one way to reach the hearts of the older men and women and that was to educate the young people and work through them.

He decided to start a school in Marcus. It was to be the first school in Stevens County. Fred's great ambition was not only to practice medicine but to teach Indian children to read and write. Here were the little children all around him who needed to be in school every day. He went to work and made his log cabin into a schoolhouse. He made some small benches, for his cabin was quite small, and made a table which reached within two feet of the walls. On one side of the table he placed the benches and one short one at the end of the table. The other end was to be his desk. His bed served as a bench on the other side.

When word was scattered that there was going to be a real school in Marcus, great was the excitement. The children were anxious to start so Fred had no trouble getting the benches filled. Sitting on the bed was the most fun, for a white man's bed was quite a curiosity... to the little savages anyway.

The beds in their teepees were made on the ground and were made of robes or skins from wild animals. Fred's bed had real wool blankets, something that was still a novelty in the West and to the Indians were very fascinating indeed. Of course, getting the children lined out in school was slow and very tiresome work but no more so than Fred had anticipated, so he was enjoying himself immensely. Their children were told to bring something to eat so at lunch time the tables were cleared of all books and papers, while the small boys and girls enjoyed their venison or fish and Indian bread, or whatever they had brought to school. Fred took the opportunity to teach them their first lesson in table etiquette.

To Fred's surprise and great satisfaction, he found that the women were very anxious to send their children to school; first, from curiosity, then, because they became interested in what the children were learning and last, but not least, because it was a good way to get them out of the way and have them well cared for besides. The little girl he had saved from drowning was one of his steadfast pupils. But Fred soon found to his dismay, that Blue Bird, for it was she, was stone deaf. He felt very sorry for her and did all he could to teach her. Her deafness made it impossible for her to learn the English language and when one day she failed to appear at her place in school, Fred understood. He said nothing but his heart ached for the little girl who loved to look at the books and was denied the chance to learn to read them.

It was not long until some of the young people began coming to him with their ailments. When they found that his remedies really helped them they began to look on him as almost super-human. That was more homage than Fred cared for. He knew that it would take time to clear away all the obstacles that littered the pathway to perfect understanding with the Indians. One day he pulled a tooth for a white man relieving him of a bad tooth ache. After that he found that people were coming to him more and more for different ailments. During school, he used his dentist chair to sit in and the table for his desk. When anyone came to him with a bad tooth the chair changed hands and the school teacher became a dentist while the children stood back and watched him pull a tooth, which by the way, was more much more exciting than studying books.

It was hard to be a teacher, doctor and dentist all at the same time. After several years of very successful work, Fred thought that he should turn his job of teaching over to others who had arrived from outside and were as capable of carrying on the good work as he was.

He was now free to put all his time in attending to the sick. This was the kind of work he really loved the most and he was soon a very busy doctor. If anyone was seriously ill he not only gave them medicine to take but went to their homes and saw that they took it, often nursing them back to health.

In that time and place there were very few people who were educated well enough to handle any business problems. It was not long until Fred, who was called "Doc Perkins" by those who knew him best, had found a new outlet for his stock of knowledge. A lawyer was badly needed to settle a case. Fred's opinion was asked and it was discovered that he had studied law and had books to prove his case. After that he was often called on when a lawyer was needed.

Fred still watched over his little school although it was being held in another building by now. He was pleased to see that they were doing well under their new teacher. Most of them now spoke English well and had learned a lot about reading and writing. In fact, he found that they excelled in writing and drawing. They were gifted with a keen imagination and light supple fingers and adapted themselves very quickly to the feel of the pen and pencil. Watching them advance was a great pleasure to Fred. To see them change from ignorant savages into civilized beings was something like watching a useless looking plant blossom into a beautiful flower, like watching the light of God penetrating the deep darkness of oblivion. He felt that he had accomplished a great lot with them.

But the grown people were much harder to reach. They had been disillusioned by the unscrupulous white people who had come before who, instead of being builders of character, had brought them much misery and suffering by teaching them and their young folks the many degrading things they knew and practiced. Along with the savage ways the Indians already possessed, they acquired the habit of drinking and often to great excess. Some of them became such drunkards that they would trade anything they had for fire water, their name for whiskey. There was no limit to their thirst for they had no regard for the consequences. Many of them were very dangerous when drunk, even though they may be just the opposite when sober.

Then came their passion for gambling. It did not take them long to learn to play cards and to catch on to the many other gambling devices the white people taught them. They had a game of their own which never seemed to lose its popularity. It was called the "stick game" or "bone game."

Two long poles were laid on the ground about three feet apart. To make it more comfortable, blankets or robes were spread out and extended on each side of the two contesting groups of players who sat facing each other alongside the two poles. Someone would start an Indian melody which was quickly taken up by both teams and carried on throughout the game while they kept time by beating on the poles with stout sticks. Whatever they cared to stake on the game was piled out in the front or between the poles so all could see what was to be gained or lost, whatever the case may be. Sometimes it would be a small amount and sometimes more according to how much they wanted to take chances on. Anyone could bet whether they played or merely looked on.

One would start the game by going through many bewildering motions, swinging his or her arms around, crossing them, lifting them high above his head and putting them behind his back, then back in front of him, then held on his lap or under his shirt if he had one, and out again, as he waved both tightly closed fists before the eyes of the intensely eager watchers, crossing them swiftly back and forth until someone guessed which hand held a small bone or stick. This was what told whether he was the winner or loser of all that was at stake for all the team. In this way, many a visiting team or tribe would carry away so much in their winnings that the losers had nothing left to lose. There was no object in carrying on the game and it would automatically come to an end, much to the chagrin of the losers who still entertained hopes of winning back some of their losses which was often much more than they had to spare; such as robes, food, money or clothing.

"Why do you gamble so much?" an old professional gambler was asked by an interested spectator. "Well, I have one robe, I play stick game and then I have two robes. I play again and have four robes."

"Yes" the other answered, "but you don't always win, do you?"

"No" the Indian grinned, "sometimes I lose. Once I was going to buy a horse. I saw some Indians playing the stick game. I thought now I will go and play stick game and win and then I can get two horses. So, I sat down and played. But when I had played just a little I left."

"Why did you leave? Did you get enough to buy two

horses?"

The Indian laughed, "No" he replied. "I left because they wouldn't play with me anymore. I had nothing to gamble with and now I don't have anything to buy even one horse with."

One old woman who had given up the habit confessed her reason for doing so. "I was very foolish about gambling," she said. "I would gamble every night. I would work hard all day, washing and ironing for the men at the garrison. Then when night came, I would take my earnings and gamble with them. Sometimes I won, but often I lost. It seemed that the more I gambled the worse I became. If I won I was so happy I wanted to gamble some more. If I lost I was very angry and wanted to gamble until I had won back what I had lost. One day I gambled everything I owned: my best clothes, my dishes, my food and even my bed was gone. That night my husband, tired from hunting all day without any luck, came home. He was hungry but there was nothing to eat. That was bad! But when it was bedtime, I had to confess that there was no bed to sleep in. We sat down side by side to wait for morning. There I was, huddled in a dark corner with plenty of time to think. I was cold and miserable and it seemed that morning would never come. My husband got up and walked out. I was lonesome. My husband left me and I didn't blame him a bit. Then he came back. In his hands, he carried his horse blanket. I thought 'now he can sleep' but no! He came and wrapped the warm blanket around my shivering body. 'Now,' he said, 'you go to sleep.' I was ashamed and it was his kindness that cured me!"

There was one thing Fred found hard to explain to the Indians and that was Christianity. "Why is it that you don't believe in God?" one Indian was asked one day. "You worship a great spirit, but it does nothing to help you whenever you are in trouble. If you believe in God, he will help you if you ask Him."

"No," the Indian replied sternly. "We do not like white man's God. White man's God is not what they say. White man catch Indian with long rope. Drag him until he is dead, and all the time, he's talking to his God."

"Oh, yes! I know what you mean," Fred replied, "You mean that the white man swears."

"Maybe," the Indian answered shaking his head. "Maybe you call it swearing but when the white man is very angry he calls on his God and when he is praying he calls on his God, too. We do not understand you."

Fred knew that the Indian was right. The white man's mind and ideas were too complicated. They were not consistent in their teachings, nor cooperative. While some of them were working daily to civilize the Indians, others were making savages out of Indians who were gifted with brighter minds and higher ideals than many of the white people themselves possessed. It was no

wonder that the Indians found the white man's
ways so hard to understand.

CHAPTER XI   Romance

There have been many stories told of the Indian people, stories that are thrilling and often very exciting. Stories told about when the white people came to America and conquered the wild Indians for land which they felt was theirs by right of possession. Stories were told about the cruelty of the Indians, their horrible scalp lifting and their terrible massacres, not bothering much to tell both sides of the two-sided story, perhaps because one side alone was shocking enough without telling the other side. Stories told, some of which were true, and many which were greatly exaggerated, most of them told in deep and prideful appreciation for the conqueror, but seldom with any understanding for the conquered who loved America first.

But in spite of everything, as time went on the Indians were finally forced by the stronger willpower and still stronger thunder weapon to unbend and surrender to the invaders. It was very hard to give up so much that they had always held so dear, such as their freedom and way of life. Once it was done, most of the Indians tried to settle down and make the best of it, but not Grey Cloud. He did not go on the warpath anymore simply because it was useless, but to forget was impossible and to forgive was not easy since no one had asked for forgiveness and never would and he knew he would not forgive if they did.

He was now living in his teepee not far from Marcus. Fred often saw him and recognized him.

He would have been on more friendly terms with
him but Grey Cloud never would relent and
continued to repulse every effort of friendliness
that Fred offered. They left each other alone as
much as possible and that was perfectly agreeable
to Grey Cloud, that is until fate took a hand.

Here we find him sitting by the fire in his teepee
smoking his long pipe and evidently dreaming of
the past, which he often did. Falling Leaf was
sitting on the other side of the fire sewing on some
moccasins. They were for Blue Bird and would be
beautiful when finished. Falling Leaf's mother had
just finished smoking the buckskin and was still
working on another deer hide which would furnish
more moccasins or gloves. She often sold gloves to
the men at the garrison who usually paid well for
them. It was really hard work making the buckskin
and a little cash was always welcome. To make a
buckskin, it was necessary to first soak the hides in
a tub of clear water until it was soft enough to
work. Then the hair was scraped off. If there was
no tub or basket at hand the hides could be soaked
in any running stream that may be near. Then if a
tree had fallen and lay in such a position that the
butt of it was just the right height from the ground,
depending on the tanner, or if she wanted to sit
down while at work, she was ready for the hides.
After the hides were well soaked and softened in
the water they were brought out and vigorously
rubbed back and forth across or over the tree butt
until both sides were entirely stripped of all the
hair, meat and grease. If there happened to be no
fallen tree handy, the work must all be done by

scraping with a smooth flat and sharp edged rock while the hides were stretched between two trees standing close together. After this was done, the hides would again be put out to soak but this time it must be in a container, generally made of birch bark and pitch, in which was water and well-rotted brains of the deer. When they had soaked in the solution for a week or more, they were taken out and stretched very tightly between two trees and once more scraped with the sharp stones until there was not a particle of waste on them.

After they had worked on a hide until it was clean and dry and had become smooth and soft from much handling, it was taken down and was ready for use. It was buckskin and could be used for many things where white buckskin was preferred. But if they wanted it smoked, which makes it much easier to clean as it does not get stiff when washed, a small fire was built of green wood with a frame over it made of green willows in the form of a small teepee. The buckskin was spread over the frame and carefully watched and often turned, its folds spread so that every inch could get the benefit of the smoke until it was evenly smoked and had become a light, medium or dark brown, whichever was preferred. It was then ready for use. The older and tougher the deer had been, the thicker and stronger the buckskin was, and better for men's moccasins.

Many of the white men who had left homes in the East to make a new start in the West had become so separated from all old ties that they had almost forgotten that they had friends or relatives other than those who were with them. Consequently, many of the young men who were free, became interested in the Indian girls and, after becoming acquainted with them, found them very intelligent and sweet. After living a number of years surrounded by Indians, where they associated with them constantly, they grew to be something like them in their likes and dislikes, in their way of living and even grew to care for them. Many of them married the Indian girls. Sometimes they lived in teepees with them like the Indians or sometimes in log cabins as the white people did.

The Indian girls often made good industrious wives for they generally were anxious to please and very quickly adapted themselves to the ways of the white man, making good housewives as they usually adapted as far as possible to the white woman's way of cooking and dressing. Many of the white men who married Indian girls were quite comfortable and happy in their chosen way of living but, as in so many walks of life, some were satisfied and some were not. Some of the white men made good husbands and some of the Indian girls made good wives and others did not, but their responsibilities were not easy to shift since divorce courts were few and far between.

Many of the Indians objected to white men marrying their girls because, for one reason, the white men did not believe in paying for their wives and the Indians did. Sometimes an Indian youth would give many ponies for the girl of his choice.

Then at times, a white man with his mind on some
white girl back East would marry an Indian girl in
a marriage which was not legal according to the
law of the white people and would then leave the
girl later on, perhaps with a child or even several
little half breed tots for the Indians to care for and
raise. These men were usually the drinking and
gambling sort and had spent much of their time in
blaming her for most of their faults, in general,
making life miserable for her. But as a rule, such a
man was not mourned by his deserted wife or by
the rest of the tribe.

Fred worked among Indians and pioneers until the
people began to realize that he was fast becoming
one of their leading men. No matter what they
wanted by way of professional services, he was the
one who was called upon and seldom was his advice
questioned by anyone.

It was not always easy to settle important disputes
to the satisfaction of all concerned so Fred could
only do his best and trust the common sense of his
clients. The West, being wild and without law and
order, must get led by the men who were broad-
minded and wise enough to deal justice to all
regardless of color or nationality. So, Fred, being
both wise and broad-minded, could always be
depended on for his fairness to all concerned.

One day Fred awoke to the realization that he was
falling in love. That he, of all people, was falling in
love was almost unbelievable. He had never
experienced anything of the kind before and had

long ago decided that he was ordained to spend his whole life in single blessedness.

That evening (in 1864,) after a very busy day, he sat gazing out over the water. He had often watched the canoes skimming over the water. He had even ridden in them for he had learned to paddle them in his travels back and forth from fort to fort and to St. Louis and back. He had been dumped into the cold water more than once. Paddling a canoe, unlike rowing a boat, was a very delicate operation if you wanted to keep the canoe right side up. Any canoe coming so gracefully across the water was interesting to watch but this one held a special attraction to him. It carried someone who was becoming very dear to him and brought a smile that covered his face and drove away the weariness that had been making him feel so downhearted.

It was Blue Bird, the little deaf girl, who stepped out of the canoe with her mother and came up to the bank to meet him. She was smiling and her eyes were shining happily. She blushed furiously when he turned and started walking by her side towards the garrison where they usually bought their groceries. Her mother walked on ahead and Fred drew Blue Bird to one side of the trail where he took Her hand and whispered in his straightforward way, " Blue Bird, will you marry me?" He spoke in the Indian language for she could not speak English.

"Yes" she answered him in the same tone of voice

as she dropped her eyes while a smile of happiness
swept over her face. She had loved Fred, it seemed,
all her life but only her mother knew of the aching,
hopelessness that her love had caused her. That a
man like Fred could ever love her, an Indian girl,
was not to be thought of, and she was really
ashamed of her secret love. After the two women
had finished their trading, they all walked down to
the river bank and Fred asked the girl if he could
come and see her very soon.

Great was his surprise when she shook her head,
the radiant smile leaving her face almost instantly,
replaced by a look of abject fear. He glanced at her
mother. The startled look on her face confirmed his
fears. He would not be welcome in their home.
After all, he knew that this should not have come
as too great a surprise, knowing so well Grey
Cloud's intense hatred of all white people. But Fred
made up his mind that he was taking no chances on
losing her and that sooner or later he was going to
see her home regardless of any trouble it might
cost.

Several days later, Blue Bird and her mother again
crossed the river, this time to bring some clothes to
the men at the Garrison whose laundry they did
each week. Fred hastened to meet them and he
knew by the smile on the mother's face that she
knew of the love Fred and Blue Bird had for each
other and approved of it.

Blue Bird looked beautiful to him as she stood
waiting for him. She was clad in a light-colored

buckskin dress trimmed with fringe and a few colored beads. Her dark thick hair hung in two heavy braids down her back reaching below her slender waistline. On her small dainty feet were a pair of beaded buckskin moccasins. She made a lovely picture as she stood amongst the tall pine trees, her face lit up with a sweet smile of welcome. It was in the evening and Fred was through for the day so he went with them as they went about doing their trading. After they were through, he surprised them by saying in very determined way, "I'm going home with you tonight!"

Blue Bird glanced at her mother with an expression of alarm spread over her face. "You can go just a little way," her mother answered for her.

"But why just a little way?" He asked, a little bit hurt.

"Just a little way," the mother replied firmly.

"All right," Fred agreed, shaking his head in a bewildered way. "A little way is better than nothing."

So, the older woman took the canoe across the river. Fred took Blue Bird across in his boat. Then he walked with them until they were in sight of their house. Falling leaf, with a friendly wave of her hand, left the two young folks to themselves, but Blue Bird was very quiet and uneasy after her mother left. Fred sensed that she had a very definite reason for worry and did not tarry long as he did not want to cause her any trouble.

With a heavy heart, he bid his sweetheart good night and she left him standing there, watching her as she went on getting to their home about the same time her mother did. Of course, Fred noticed all this but thought nothing of it for he had heard a lot about Grey Cloud in his younger days and, by what he had seen of him, he did not think he had changed any in the past years. He still carried a grudge against the white people and Fred knew that his hatred for them burned fiercely in his heart as in his younger days, yet he knew that nothing good could come of her mother keeping the girl away from him, for he loved her and was determined that nothing in the world would induce him to give her up as long as she returned that love.

Since the death of Eagle Eye, Grey Cloud had cared for his wife and three girls, besides the two boys of his own, and had provided well for them. The mother of the two boys had been dead for many years and Grey Cloud had never remarried, probably because in his younger life he had never remained in one place long enough. Whatever his reasons were, he was contented to spend the rest of his life just as he was.

The only trouble he seemed to have with his young folks was that he could not prevent them from associating with white people, much as he hated it, but the white people were teaching his young folks to read and write and he had to admit that he thought that was a good thing. Blue Bird and her sister did not share his opinion of the white people. They could see where these people with their strange ways had made life much more interesting to them. Blue Bird, who had learned to understand them, could see where the white people had done a lot towards bringing a new and better way of living to them and now she was planning to marry Fred. She was sure that not all the white people were bad.

The three sisters were nothing alike in disposition. Owl Eyes, the oldest girl was a sullen and disagreeable girl with a grafting selfish nature. She never missed a chance to take advantage of her more gentle sisters and was generally disobedient and ungrateful to her mother and uncle.

Blue Bird and Red Wing were both kind and considerate with all their associates and were dearly loved by all. Red Wing, who was the youngest of the three, loved Blue Bird so loyally that she would do anything for her, counting nothing too hard or disagreeable. Falling Leaf had often said that Red Wing would willingly have gone through fire and water for her sister.

Fred knew that Owl Eyes did not like him any better than her uncle did and would be just as quick to make him trouble if the opportunity ever presented itself, but why she did not like him was what puzzled him. Perhaps it was because he did not like her. He knew that Red Wing and her mother were his friends and that helped a lot, but

he knew that with so much prejudice against him
they could do very little to help him should he find
that the anxiety for the safety of his sweetheart
proved not to be groundless.

Owl Eyes was in high spirits when her mother and
Blue Bird arrived home that night. This was
something very unusual for Owl Eyes was seldom
good-natured, especially if left to do the work at
home. But tonight, she had supper all ready and
was hurrying around getting it on the table. Her
mother smiled happily, for she was well pleased
with her wayward daughter, but one thing troubled
her. "Where did you get all that fresh meat and all
the other good thing you have?" She asked
anxiously.

"Oh," Owl Eyes answered, glancing slyly towards
the door. "I was lucky today and earned a little
money at the Block House so I brought home
something for supper."

"How nice," her mother replied highly pleased, as
she thought to herself, "Perhaps I have never
understood my oldest daughter or maybe she has
decided to do better." But a moment later her face
fell and her heart grew heavily with
disappointment for she knew her daughter had
deceived her once more. She had lied to her. Nick
Rider came in from the barn and she knew that it
was he who had brought the groceries, as he had
done before when he came to visit them. Nick Rider
was a man of about 35 who had taken up a
homestead a few miles away somewhere in the hills

north of Colville. He liked to come and see them. As he never appeared to take any special notice of the girls, the uncle was always glad to see him, thinking it was he in whom the man was interested. He loved to hear the many stories the man told, for he was a Spaniard and had traveled a lot.

But Falling Leaf did not trust him and she did not believe that he had come to see her brother with three pretty girls around. She did not like the idea of him coming to see them. Then, as if in answer to her depressing thoughts the man removed all doubts of his intentions concerning her daughters. This evening he seemed unable to keep his admiring glances from straying in the direction of the girls, especially Blue Bird. Then, to the disgust of the girl, he took the seat next to her at the table. Blue Bird blushed furiously and, with hot anger seething in her heart, she arose from the table and allowed her understanding mother to take her place. Nick did not appear to mind or even notice the slight, but Red Wing noticed with an anxious feeling that Owl Eyes laughed merrily at her sister's discomfort. She did not like the grin that swept over Nick's face nor did she like his familiarity in their home.

He was a white man and Red Wing thought that Owl Eyes was too friendly with him and allowed him too many privileges. She was young but she knew that nice young girls did not get so familiar with men like Nick Rider. He was generally considered a man of undesirable reputation, a reputation earned by his love for strong drink. He always carried a gun but was never known to have used it in a fight, although he was generally pretty ugly around men when drunk. He was tall and slender with long black curly hair which hung around his shoulders. He always wore boots and spurs, cowboy hat and other cowboy regalia including a well filled cartridge belt with his big ugly revolver hanging from it strapped down and always ready for instant use. He owned a large herd of cattle and did well at the business for there was plenty of pasture free to all who wished to profit by it. Living away up in the hills with no neighbors to molest him, he had all the hills of Colville for pasture land and made it his business to raise and sell beef to men at the garrison. He made plenty of money so he usually dressed well and, much to the amusement of Blue Bird and Red Wing, wore shiny gold earrings. These earrings always caused the two girls to whisper and do a lot of giggling but he did not mind it. He would only smile for, with all his faults, he was never anything around the ladies but extremely polite, even when drunk, a habit which caused many to retain a feeling of respect for him at all times.

He was not handsome. In fact, had he been less particular about his appearance, he would have very easily been just the opposite. Unfortunately for him he had but one eye which always emphasized his reputation of being a bold bad man, a reputation scarcely deserved since his worst faults were drinking and bragging about his many imaginary conquests in battle. He feared no man

187

whether he was drunk or sober but his skillfulness with the gun caused many to fear him. He was conceited enough to be proud of the fact. Cattle thieves were plentiful and he had need of his skill and his reputation as a number one shot. It often saved him the necessity of being forced to use more drastic measures in order to protect his herds.

But no matter how skillful a man may be, or what sort of business he may be most accomplished in, he is sure to meet his match someday and a man is very apt to reap whatever he sows.

CHAPTER XII   California

In the little home near Marysville, California, the
Wynecoop family had almost ceased to think of the
home they had left in the East[4]. They were busy
building their new home. Curtis had grown to be
quite a big boy now and seemed to find plenty to
keep him busy. He never regretted coming West.
Young as he was, the West was all that a boy could
desire. He hated crowds of people and he hated city
life. He loved the wide-open spaces and loved to
help his father care for the pigs and cattle. In fact,
he loved everything in the West but best of all he
loved the cowboys. There were plenty of cowboys in
the West and the one great ambition growing in the
heart of the boy was to be a real cowboy. He was too
young to do much riding so he practiced on the cows
and pigs. He found that it was not very easy to stay
on a pig's back and quite often Curt, as he was
called, would find himself sitting on the ground or
in a mud puddle, which was often the case, while
the pig would be somewhere else trying to keep out
of his reach.

But riding cows was his real hobby. Nothing
pleased him more than to stick to some real
troublesome calf. He was usually pretty good at it
but occasionally he would find one that was too
much for him.

His mother had one calf that she had strictly

---

[4] (1865)

forbidden him to ride. The calf was wild and strong. She was afraid for him to try it. She wanted it tamed, so Curt thought it could be broke to ride. The idea that there was a calf in the corral that his mother was afraid for him to ride hurt his pride. He thought anybody ought to be able to ride a calf and he was determined to show his doubting mother that he could.

He tried several times but the wily calf would not let him get on. One day when he thought no one was looking, he decided that he must show the calf that he was boss. He felt that if there was a single calf on the place that he couldn't ride, he could never hope to be a bronc buster. He couldn't be a cowboy unless he was a good rider. Watching for a good chance, he sprang onto the back of the unsuspecting calf. Instantly the surprised animal gave a lively leap and went into action, bucking, bawling and kicking up its heels in a way that threatened to unseat him every time at every jump. Around and around they went until the calf made a dash for the barn. Then Curt remembered too late that the calf was tied to a long rope and, before he could even think, he was flying through the air in highly approved cowboy style, landing in a heap on, of all things, a broken bottle. His hand was so badly cut that there was nothing to do but go to the house and have his mother bandage it for him and tell her what happened.

She first bound up his lacerated and bleeding hand, then gave him a sound spanking for disobeying her, but she did not forbid him to ride anymore!

Not long after that, he was given a gentle horse to ride which pleased him greatly except for one thing: the horse was too gentle, and after all, riding a gentle horse was tame business after having experienced the thrill of trying to stay on the backs of pigs and cows.

Then one day he accepted the job of herding a large herd of hogs. He was to watch them and keep them from wandering too far away from home. Herding them on horseback was rather difficult so that gave him a perfect excuse for riding the hogs. It was much harder to break a hog to ride than a calf because they are much harder to stick to. Herding hogs on hogback was quite exciting and much more satisfactory than riding a nice gentle horse. He finally did manage to break in an old hog to ride, one that was big and strong, and trained him to be a real service to him. He rode the hog wherever the herd led him and never needed to worry about his mount leaving him afoot. If he wanted to get off and walk a while, the old hog was always ready for him, needing no saddle or bridal. If he wanted a little excitement to pass away the time, there was always other hogs to break.

There were a lot of snakes around there but they did not worry Curt as long as he stayed near the hogs. They ate every snake they found, no matter if they were rattlers or other dangerous snakes. Sometimes there were exciting times too, if the snake in desperation tried to escape.

After herding hogs for a while he took a job herding cattle. This was not much fun, for now he was obliged to ride his gentle horse and was not allowed to ride the calves. The cattle were not hard to watch for the country was comparatively level and they could not easily get lost.

One day he was looking for a calf in the tulles, a swamp covered with cat tails or tulles as they were generally called. There was a number of tulle lakes around and occasionally a calf would get lost in one. Curt noticed smoke at the farther end of the swamp as he went in but he did not let that stop him although he well knew just how dangerous a swamp fire could be. He hurriedly began searching and, as luck would have it, found the calf in a few moments. As he hastened to leave the tulles he could see the black smoke reaching high above the swamp. He knew in a few minutes he would be in a blazing inferno and the safest thing for him to do was to leave the calf and run as fast as he could. The calf, contrary to most cattle, seemed to understand the dangers that threatened them and made straight for the edge of the swamp, which they reached just in time to save themselves.

The rest of the cattle, not liking the heat nor the looks of the fire, wandered a short distance away. The calf was soon with its mother where it stayed while Curt drove them back to better pasture, feeling pretty lucky that they were all alive and safe.

John did not try prospecting this time as the Gold

Rush appeared to be over in the valley and the
mining claims were practically all taken up.
Besides that, John had already proved to himself
that he was not a very good miner during the gold
rush days in '49. A mining camp, in his opinion,
was a poor place for a man with a family anyway.
He was not sorry that he had brought his family
out West but he often thought of the comfortable
home they had left back East and wondered if he
had been wise in leaving it to come so far from
civilization, good schools and doctors.

He could not seem to make much money at farming
and since they had found themselves almost
penniless after a long and hard journey across the
plains and the added expense of getting settled in
their new home, there was nothing to do but to find
something else to do where he could make some
money. He got a job freighting. This took him away
from home a good part of the time and, in his
travels, he found many opportunities for looking
the country over. This he did and finally decided
that California was not the only rich state in the
union. One time while spending a few weeks in
Nevada he saw that there was some good land that
had not been taken. He decided to stake a claim to
some of it. He was quite proud of his new
possession and hoped someday to give Mandy and
the children a very nice surprise. He worked on the
place whenever he had a chance to do so but such
opportunities were pretty scarce since he still had a
job to do. Mandy found it pretty hard to keep their
large family clothed and fed on the money John
was able to earn so she went to work too, doing any

kind of work that she could find to do. She was a natural born doctor and was often called on for help if anyone in the neighborhood became ill. She was also a fine nurse and made a few dollars by nursing her patients back to health. This fact often helped her and saved her much worry about her own family too. She knew many remedies that could be prepared at home without much experience. Of course, she was not a professional doctor so she could not practice except in emergency cases. Being so far from any doctor she was always more than welcome in any sick room to do all she could, sometimes saving a life.

By earning a few cents wherever she could and by practicing the strictest economy the family managed to exist. Mandy at times longed for the old folks and the home in the East where John was seldom away from home and where she was always home with the children instead of being away working, as she often was these days.

Then she would remember how beautiful the West was for those who were fortunate enough to be settled in homes of their own, some of them lovely homes, for many of the people were doing quite well and were proof that the West kept its promise to some of them at least and she did not forget that it held many wonderful promises for them too, if they could only stay with it. This made her all the more determined to keep on working and waiting for their dream to come true.

She often heard of other settlements where people

were even less fortunate than they were, where many were almost destitute with scarcely enough food to keep body and soul together with no alternative but to bear the hardships until they could get a fast hold in a country where, owing to their trouble with the Indians, a foothold would be precarious at best. "At least we are not troubled with Indians anymore and we've never really been down and out yet," Mandy thought. Nevertheless, the West had not proved to be the land of plenty they had expected it to be, although there was no denying the fact that it still gave great promise of becoming all they had expected of it, if they could only outlive the discouragements. Mandy was a good house keeper and nothing was ever wasted. Nothing was ever to lay idle if it could be made useful. She was a good seamstress and, when at home, was always spinning or sewing something for the children. Added to this, with the help of the children, they ground their own meal for mush or bread and were soon raising their own fruit and vegetables which did much to keep them from ever being in actual want.

There were hundreds of acres of good farming land just as the report had come to them while in the East. Instead of so much land to be taken free, they found that most of the best land had already been taken and they had been obliged to take what they could get, which was not enough for extensive farming and not nearly as much as they had expected or hoped to get. But it made them a nice little home and they tried to be satisfied and make the best of it. In spite of their disappointment they still loved the Golden West.

Then came their first real trouble. Lizzie, who never had been very robust, began failing in health. Mandy did everything she could think of, tried every remedy within her store of knowledge, but all during the winter Lizzie gradually faded away and when the March winds began to blow in the spring, she passed away. This was a sad blow to John and Mandy for they realized that the West with its many hardships had been too hard on their little daughter and they blamed themselves for her death. The family, bruised by the loss of their loved one, pushed on trying hard in the face of so many obstacles to be cheerful and brave, but other worries kept them busy and there was not much time for grieving. John was finding it harder as time went on to get work. His expenses were so heavy that he could make no headway at all. Then, just when things began brightening up a little and they were beginning to feel that there were prospects of better times ahead, John came home sick. He had been unable to get back up into Nevada where his rich claims were and was still hoping for time and opportunity to prove their worth before he told Mandy about them, but now that he was not getting any better he decided to let her in on his little secret. He gave her the numbers and told her about the place, where it was located and what a wonderful home he thought it would make now that the boys were old enough to farm it. Mandy did all she could for John but it was all to no avail. She worked night and day with him, never leaving his bedside unless absolutely necessary but he grew worse and finally, for the second time within a few short years, death claimed her loved one.

After John was laid to rest, Mandy was utterly discouraged. She blamed the West for all their troubles, knowing so well that it was hard work and lack of care that caused his death, the same thing that had taken her little daughter not long before, but there was nothing that could be done about it. They now had no money with which to return to the East even if they had wanted to. She felt that after all this time she would have no place to go anyway, if she did go back. Her father and mother were no longer living, neither were John's folks. She knew there was no other place to go, and she knew too that, like John had been, she and her family were part of the West from now on and there was no turning back. But life has a way of making poor discouraged mortals go right on living and hoping, sometimes in the face of despair, danger and deprivation, for a bit of sunshine and happiness never before encountered and often they are rewarded for their perseverance in unexpected ways. Their life in the little California home went on. The children were growing up now and all were doing well in school, thanks to Mandy's good management and would soon be making their own way in the world.

Curt was now a young man of 20, and was busy in helping his mother in every way possible, but he was getting restless and often coaxed his mother to move to Oregon. Some of his friends had settled

there and gave excellent reports of the country;
that is all good reports but one, that the Indians
were forever going on the war path up there, but
that was all that was necessary to keep Mandy
perfectly satisfied to remain in California for the
rest of her life. She had never forgotten their
terrible experiences on the plains, and was sure
that she would never care to see another Indian as
long as she lived. Indians, to many of the white
people, were something only meant to be
exterminated, with no intelligence and no souls, for
why else would they prey on the white people? The
idea that the Indians had rights in this wonderful
country even though they didn't consider
themselves the rightful owners of it, did not enter
the white man's heads. These were the sentiments
of most of the invaders including Mandy. Upon
hearing that many white men in Oregon were
marrying Indian girls, she was terribly shocked and
declared that if one of her boys ever did such a
thing, she could not disown him fast enough. "Of
course," she would say, "my boys would never do
such a crazy thing and besides they were old
enough to remember the massacre on the plains.
They know how horrible the Indians can be."

It was about this time that Ed[5] decided to go to
Nevada and look up his father's land claim. When
he got there, it was only a short time until he had
located the numbers John had given them, but
another man had taken advantage of John's
absence and had settled there. He had changed the

---

[5] Curt's brother(?) ed.

numbers and when Ed and found the place marked with the numbers he carried, it was nothing but a rock pile. Ed knew that his father had been cheated out of his property, but he felt there was nothing to be done about it so he went back home. Since they had never seen the place before and had not even known of it until recently, it was not too much of a disappointment to Mandy. That anyone could be so mean as to cheat a sick man was more than she could understand. At any rate, she felt that if it was to be that way, it was better John had never known of it, for it would have broken his heart to find that all his efforts to provide something better for the future had been all in vain

CHAPTER XIII   In The Mountains

[6]When Blue Bird left the table, she went outdoors and hurried down to the river where she sat on the bank watching the moonbeams playing on the shimmering blue waters. She was thinking of Fred, wondering what he was doing and if he were thinking of her.

She was lonely and she could not understand why, for she had been with him such a short time before. She knew that Owl Eyes and Nick were laughing, talking and having a good time, probably at her expense. She was wondering what Owl Eyes could see about him to like. She thought of his apparent interest in her and shuddered. She wished that he would forget about her, then she laughed softly to herself, "Those earrings," she thought. "They are so funny." Then her thoughts returned to the happenings of the day and she blushed as she remembered the words of love Fred had spoken to her. "Love." She had never known before what the word meant. She was too young to know now but nevertheless she did and her brown eyes shone brightly while her tender lips trembled into a sweet smile of happiness. Suddenly without warning, a heavy blanket was thrown over her head! Startled, she struggled wildly and screamed. Instantly a heavy hand covered her mouth, then she felt herself being carried up the river bank. Strong arms held her in a vice like grip, holding her so

---

[6] (c.1864)

closely that she struggled for breath, afraid that she would smother.

She was becoming more frightened each moment, for she had no idea what was happening to her or where she was being taken. She only knew that she was being carried away from the river.

"But, why?" Then she felt herself being lowered and then laid onto something soft and warm. Ropes were being wrapped around her and she knew they were being tied by her abductor, whoever he or she may be.

A few moments passed and then she felt a movement under her and knew that she was traveling. Someone was taking her away somewhere in a wagon. Instinctively she knew who it was as well as if she could see or hear him. It was Nick Rider for he was the only one she knew who owned a wagon and was interested in her in any way. Now she knew why he had come to her uncle's cabin so often.

She struggled frantically until her arms were sore from straining against the stout ropes, but she found that it was useless for she could not get away. Finally, she gave up trying and spent the time crying miserably; the heartbreaking sobs shaking her slight form until she became so weary that she fell into a light sleep. They traveled all night, Blue Bird spending most of the time in bitter weeping. When morning came and the girl could feel the warm sun beating down on her, the wagon stopped. She felt that someone was coming near her. Then, whoever it was picked her up in his arms. She tried to jerk away from him, but soon found that to be impossible, so tightly was she held. She almost wished that she could die and thought "If only my mother, Red Wing or Fred would come." She never once thought of Owl Eyes or her uncle as protectors for she never trusted them. Whoever was carrying her, finally put her down on what felt like a bed. Then the blanket was pulled off her face and she looked up into the grinning face of Nick Rider, just as she had surmised. Very gently he removed the ropes. "How do you feel?" he asked in the Indian language. Ignoring his question, Blue Bird sprang to her feet. "Why am I here?" she asked, her dark eyes glazing angrily.

"You are here because I brought you here. This is my home," he answered smilingly.

"That does not concern me!" Blue Bird answered, as tears of rage rolled down her pale cheeks.

"Oh, yes it does concern you," he replied smilingly, "because it is your home, too. You belong to me now, don't you see?"

"No, no!" the frightened girl screamed in desperation. "I wouldn't belong to you no matter what you say! No matter what anyone says."

"Oh, yes you would," Nick replied, "because Owl Eyes, your own sister, sold you to me so you can't help yourself. I gave her a lot of pretty cloth and beads, besides a quarter of beef for you, and now, no matter whether you are worth it or not, you belong to me, sweetheart."

Blue Bird sank back onto the bed and sat there while the full realization of her plight dawned on her. Had her sister really done this to her? How could any sister have been so heartless? But still, when she thought of it, she was not too surprised for Owl Eyes had never shown her a moments kindness as far back as she could remember.

Nick left her while he went out to attend to his horses.

No sooner had the door closed than she was trying eagerly to open it, but it was bolted so all her efforts were in vain. She looked around for the first time and saw that she was in a log cabin with the windows boarded up, making escape seem impossible.

She was broken hearted. That fate could play such a trick on her was almost unbelievable. She knew that she was literally a prisoner, and she had never harmed a person in her life. In a very short time Nick returned to the cabin. He appeared to be well satisfied with this night's work. "Hungry?" He asked quite cheerily. Blue Bird shook her head angrily, as she gazed longingly out the one small window which was not completely boarded up.

"Oh, yes you are!" He said smiling.

The girl glared at him too angry to speak. In a few minutes, Nick had a fire burning brightly and he was whistling merrily as he began cooking breakfast. Blue Bird was determined not to eat anything, although she was very hungry after her night-long journey. In a short time, Nick came to her with a steaming hot breakfast of hotcakes, coffee and well-cooked steak. Blue Bird glanced at it and shook her head. "Come now!" Nick said sternly. "You must eat something. I know you are hungry and we are not going back for a long time. You know I love you, don't you?"

"No, no," the girl screamed, stomping her foot. "I don't think you love me at all. I don't love you either! I don't even like you! I hate you!"

"I know you do," the man answered quietly, "but someday you will like me. You may even learn to love me. But now you must not be afraid of me because I will be good to you, you'll see."

Thoroughly disgusted, Blue Bird turned her back on him. He brought the food and set it down beside her, then went to the table where he ate his own breakfast in silence. Blue Bird looked at the food and concluded that she would gain nothing by injuring her health and she had sense enough to know that she would need all her strength if she ever got a chance to escape for she knew that she was a long way from home and afoot. After she had finished her breakfast, Nick came and took away the dishes.

"That's a good girl," he said pleasantly. "I knew you were too brave a girl to act like a baby." He then washed the dishes and put everything in order. "I'm going to Colville," he said as he reached for his hat. "I will be back as soon as I can." Then he went out the door, glancing sidelong at her as he closed the door. Needless to say, Blue Bird was very happy to see him leave and breathed a sigh of relief as he disappeared from sight. "I'll not be here when he gets back," she thought hopefully. She forced herself to wait patiently until she felt sure that Nick must be well on his way, then she sprang quickly to the door and tried to open it. It was locked, just as she had expected. She tried to kick it open but found it was made of heavy timbers and, built so strong and fastened on the outside as it was, it was impossible to break it down. Very badly disappointed, she then tried the windows. They were heavily barred. She was becoming desperate. She was all alone, not a soul to keep her from making her escape, and she was helpless to even make a start. The cabin was built of strong solid logs, without a single weak place that she could find and to make her prison more secure Nick had left nothing in the cabin that could be used to knock a log or window bar loose. She finally decided with a sinking heart that her captor had been well prepared before bringing her to his new mountain home.

Throwing herself on the bed, she gave up in despair. Nick had left her plenty of food and water so she did not suffer physically, although she ate very little food, only as much as she could force herself to eat. The day was spent in continually trying some new way of breaking out, finding nothing that was successful. She could see through the bars across the windows that the sun was shining brightly, and that the cabin stood in the middle of a small clearing, with nothing to keep her company but mountains, heavy timber and wild animals. She could not see the wild animals but she knew they were not far off.

She waited all day for the sound or rather the vibration of the heavy wagon wheels as they rolled over the rough ground to tell her that Nick had returned, for she dreaded the time of his returning with all her heart. But as the sun went down and the heavy darkness folded around the little cabin she began to breathe easier and finally went to sleep.

She slept the sleep of a weary child and when she woke up the sun was once more streaming in through the windows. Startled, she sprang to her feet, very wide-awake and looked around. Everything was just as it had been the night before, and she knew that Nick had not returned. Another day passed exactly as had the day before and that evening, just at dusk, she felt the rumble of the wheels coming up the road. She had been dreading this, but nevertheless she felt that another day alone locked up as a prisoner would have been almost unbearable. Then the door opened and Nick stood in the doorway. Immediately, she was filled with fear and dread. She had never trusted him and now to know that he had her in his power was a terrible realization.

"Hello," was his cheery greeting. "How are you? Did you think I was never coming back or did you care if I never came back?"

Blue Bird only stared at the man without answering.

"Look here," he said with a wide grin, as he handed her a large package. "I thought you might like something with which to pass away the time so I bought you this."

Blue Bird would not touch the package and only stared in disdain at the giver.

"Oh, don't be afraid of it," he laughed. "It won't bite you." Then he opened it for her and spread it out on the bed for her to see. Blue Bird stared in surprise for he showed her some of the prettiest dress goods she had ever seen. There were also some lovely beads, earrings and other trinkets. She could scarcely keep back a smile of pleasure for she was not unlike other girls in her love for pretty things and, since her training did not prohibit her from accepting presents, she decided that even though she hated the giver she would gladly accept his gifts. Anyway, she felt that Nick really owed it to her for all the misery he had caused her so, taking them without thanking him, she shoved them under her pillow.

If Nick was disappointed in her apparent lack of

appreciation, he did not show it, as he turned and began preparing their supper. Blue Bird knew that Nick drank a lot, and had been afraid that he would return drunk, and it had been a great relief to see him walk through the doorway perfectly sober.

He was pretty quiet all during suppertime. He had first invited her to the table to sit beside him, but when she shook her head, he carefully dished out her supper and brought it to her, going back to the table and sitting with his back to her while he ate. They were both hungry and the meal was very good so they ate it with relish. When he was through with the dishes, he came and sat down beside her and began telling her about his trip to Colville. Blue Bird wished with all her heart that he would not want to be near her. He pretended not to notice her stony silence and hate filled glances and continued his friendly one-sided conversation until it began to grow late. Then taking his hat, he said, "Goodnight" and went out.

Blue Bird was so glad to see him leave that she was almost happy for a moment. It was not long until she was fast asleep in her warm and comfortable bed.

One morning Nick was getting ready to take some meat to the Garrison near Marcus. Blue Bird was getting so lonesome that she was almost sick. She knew where he was going and that he would very likely see her mother, Red Wing, and maybe Fred and she felt that she should be doing something about it. If only she could get out, she felt that she would have no trouble finding her way home but even if she never got home she knew she would be happier wherever she was than with Nick.

After breakfast Nick came and sat down beside her. She immediately moved away from him. "Blue Bird," he said kindly. "I love you. Will you marry me?" These were almost the exact words Fred had used and they struck her like a slap in the face.

CHAPTER XIV   A Friend in Need

"Why hello," Nick fairly shouted as he grasped the outstretched hand of Owl Eyes. "Come in – come in. Gosh, it's good to see you! How are you anyway, and how's Uncle Grey Cloud, the old renegade?"

Owl Eyes laughed as she stepped into the cabin, shaking Nick's hand in the old familiar way. She was watching Blue Bird as she came towards her. Blue Bird quickly looked the other way, then she caught a glimpse of Red Wing as she stood beside her horse just a short distance from the door as if undecided just what to do. She smiled at Blue Bird and Blue Bird smiled tearfully while wishing desperately that, in some way or twist of fate, she may go back with her.

Owl Eyes and Nick were apparently on very good terms and were really pleased to see each other again. Nick seemed to have so many things that he wanted to talk over and perhaps he thought that, with her sister so nearby, he could allow Blue Bird a little more freedom so he left the door open. He and Owl Eyes strolled around a bit. It seemed the two had some very serious problems to solve for they wandered some distance away while talking very earnestly all the while. Red Wing and Blue Bird smiled at each other through the doorway. Nick's wagon stood directly in front of the door and Red Wing, having mounted her pony again, rode up near the wagon tongue, meanwhile talking to Blue Bird in their usual way, mostly with hand motion.

Blue Bird could see the possibilities in the setting and her heart began beating violently as she glanced out and saw how far away were the two who were responsible for her trouble. So engrossed were they in each other and what they were talking about that it was quite evident that the two girls were for the moment completely forgotten.

Suddenly Blue Bird realized that her sister was thinking of the same thing she had in mind, for very cautiously she was motioning to her with her hand. Blue Bird nodded understandingly and began stealthily creeping from the doorway towards the wagon, then very quietly onto the tongue of the wagon, carefully keeping out of sight of the other two in the meantime. Then suddenly, with one swift leap she was on the back of the horse behind her sister and then they shot off down the trail, which for good reasons of their own, they preferred to the road which had much better traveling.

Hearing the sudden commotion of the startled horse as he galloped madly away, Owl Eyes yelled and ran for her horse. Nick ran for his horse and of course the two horses became frightened at their mad haste and it was some lengthy moments before the plunging horses would let them on their backs. Owl Eyes had noticed which way the two girls had gone so they went thundering down the trail after them. Nick was in the lead, swearing and fuming while he beat and jerked his horse by the bit trying to make him go faster.

Red Wing had a good horse and the two girls were

not very heavy so for a while the two pursuers found it impossible to gain on them. At last the two runaway girls reached the thick timber and were lost entirely to view.

Red Wing kept her pony going at full speed down the winding trail, confident that they were leaving their pursuers far behind for it was not long until she could not hear the sound of the pursuing hoof beats, but their luck was not to hold out. Their obedient pony was beginning to slow up and Red Wing decided that it would be wise to stop and listen, just for fear that their pursuers might be nearer than they thought. To her horror, she immediately discovered that her sister and Nick were gaining on them and at the rate they were traveling would soon catch up with them.

Becoming thoroughly frightened at the sound, Red Wing began to jerk on the bridal reigns and both girls jabbed their heels into the flanks of the straining pony until they knew that the poor beast could go no faster. At this rate, Blue Bird would soon be back in the cabin she was trying so hard to escape from and would undoubtedly be more closely guarded than ever. Remembering the dire threats that Nick had made if she ever tried to escape, Blue Bird was almost sick with fear.

Suddenly, with a silent motion for her to follow suit, Red Wing slid easily from the moving horse's back onto the grassy ground. Instantly Blue Bird was beside her and the two girls vanished quickly into the heavy timber and tangled underbrush, but not before Red Wing had given her pony a sharp slap on the rump which sent him tearing down the trail.

Nick and Owl Eyes were traveling so fast with their minds bent only on recapturing the two fugitives that they never thought to watch the ground for footprints, which were not very noticeable. They never even thought of the scheme the girls had in mind to trick them into following the lone pony.

The frightened animal led them several miles before the two very angry and disgruntled pursuers discovered that they had been outwitted. They went back carefully examining the trail as they went, but so sly had the girls been that they left no telltale signs behind them, not a footprint nor a broken twig, not even a crushed blade of grass to expose their hiding place. Finally, after darkness began to settle over the deep forest making it impossible for them to see even the beaten trail, the two disgusted people gave up the search.

Owl Eyes promised to do all in her power to help him find Blue Bird and the discouraged lover returned to his mountain home determined to have Blue Bird back no matter what the cost may be.

The next morning, he hitched up his team and, taking what supplies he thought he would need, went down the river to Marcus where he decided to camp near the home of the two girls until they should return there, which he figured out would not be long, for hunger and thirst would soon drive them home if he were lucky. That evening he went to see Grey Cloud. The old man did not act very friendly at first. Nick was at a loss as to what the trouble was. He was sure that the old man had approved of his bargain with Owl Eyes for Blue Bird. As he had reached Blue Bird's home before she had, knowing Owl Eyes as he did, he was sure that no one had told him of her escape, so there seemed no reason for his coolness.

Nick knew very well that losing girls, even though they be but Indian girls, was very serious business and a white man in a country inhabited by Indians stood a chance of losing his scalp for a lot less than for losing young girls. He knew too that Grey Cloud was letting him hang around there strictly for some reason of his own for he had no love for any white man and would just as soon scalp him as look at him.

Whatever Nick was, he was no coward and he decided to break the news to Grey Cloud come what may. The man was really very much concerned about the two girls for he knew that they could very easily get lost in the thick timber and besides that the mountains were infested with many kinds of wild animals.

"Blue Bird ran away," he said bluntly, in his hurry to tell of his misfortune, forgetting to speak in the Indian language as he usually did when speaking to Indians. He seated himself on the floor before the old man and began nervously filling his pipe. He expected to see the Indian blow up into a towering rage but what a surprise awaited him.

"Ho, ho, ho," the old fellow laughed, slapping his buckskin covered knee. "My girl heap smart! White man no catchum her!" Then quite suddenly the wily old man changed his tactics. Leaning towards the unsuspecting Spaniard, he whispered confidentially in his own language. "I'll tell you what we will do. I will help you catch the girls. Maybe it will take one day, maybe one week but they will get hungry and then they will come home. You stay here and watch. I will go away up in the hills and if I don't catch them, you will."

"All right," Nick agreed, glad to know that the old uncle was for him instead of against him. "I'll do whatever you say. They are bound to come here sooner or later. There's no other place for them to go."

At these words the face of the Indian grew stern. "Yes! There is another place," he answered, his dark eyes contracting in anger. "The white Doctor across the river says he is going to marry Blue Bird and every day he hunts for her. He never grows tired. He eats but very little and he never sleeps; always he hunts and hunts for my Blue Bird."

Nick knew about Blue Bird and Fred and was not surprised to hear of his worries and instantly became filled with a terrible anger. He sprang to his feet. "That man," he screamed. "If I ever get my hands on him, I'll kill him! If it wasn't for him Blue Bird would be with me today. I want to marry her and that's more than he would do. He's just like the rest of the black hearted white men. He'd be ashamed to marry an Indian girl. They're not good enough for such people."

Grey Cloud grinned cunningly. The implication that his favorite niece may not be good enough for the white doctor only served to add fuel to his growing resentment towards the angry Spaniard. He really loved his fatherless niece in his own savage way, but he had his own ideas about what was good for her, and also about what was good for himself, in a financial way, that is.

"White men no pay for pretty wife," he had been heard to grumble, "so I keep her, maybe someday catchum good husband. White doctor no can have."

In the meantime, the two girls were far up in the mountains wearily picking their painful way through the thick timber and tangled bush. It was in the summertime, so there were plenty of berries and roots. They were fortunate in finding water so they did not suffer too much from hunger or thirst.

The wilderness was a wild and dreary place for two young girls to be wandering about. What with the fear of meeting wild animals, which worried them during the daytime and frightened them so much at night, sleep was almost impossible, tired as they were. Then there was the vast loneliness that surrounded them on every side. The sudden chirping of a bird or the cracking of bush made by some animal, perhaps a harmless deer, always set their hearts to beating furiously. Blue Bird, unable to hear, was saved this ordeal to a certain extent but the fear on her sister's face was always reflected on her own. Although she had a dread of meeting wild animals, "Humans" she thought were much more to be dreaded or feared than any of the wildest animals. She knew that they could not remain out in the woods forever but she was afraid to go home knowing that long before she could even hope to reach there, Owl Eyes would be there waiting for her, and Nick would be there too, waiting with open arms.

Horrors! The thought of meeting that man again sent chills up and down her back and almost made her wish that she could die. It made the fear of the wild animals seem like nothing in comparison. One thought haunted her continually, if she could only see Fred! He would save her. He would advise her what to do. He would save... not only her life, but her soul, for her soul meant nothing to Nick.

Red Wing did not fear either Nick or Owl eyes. She had outwitted both of them before and she could do it again. So, the girls, after many days of wandering over the hills hungry and tired out, with worn-out moccasins and torn dresses, found themselves walking on familiar ground once more. To Blue Bird's surprise, Red Wing led her to where a canoe was hidden in the brush along the river bank.

"I'm afraid to go home," she said, "so we will go to Marcus first. There we will hide until we can decide

what to do next. I know Fred will help us. He has
been like a wild man since you left. I think he
would like to kill that one-eyed Spaniard. But
never fear, that man will never get his dirty hands
on you again. I'll see to that!"

They crossed the river under cover of darkness and
once more Red Wing remembered to hide the canoe
in the brush away from prying eyes. They soon
found the trail that led down to Marcus. It was
morning when they reached their destination and a
very short time later they were at Fred's cabin
door. At Red Wing's timid knock, Fred opened the
door. He was pale and hollow-eyed, utterly
discouraged after the many days of searching for
his little sweetheart. One glance told him who his
early-morning visitors were and he sprang forward
with a glad cry of welcome. "Blue Bird! My darling,"
he exclaimed joyously. "Where did you come from?
How did you get here? We have been searching
everywhere for you! Oh my dear, how glad I am to
see you." He almost shouted as he clasped her in
his arms. Then seeing the uneasy look in the eyes
of her sister and noticing how tired and hungry the
girls looked, he hurriedly drew them inside and
closed the door. "We must not let anyone see you,"
he whispered, remembering that others might see
them and report the news to their uncle.

In a very short time Fred had something set out for
them to eat and, afterward, he insisted that he and
Blue Bird be married at once. "We must take no
more chances," he said anxiously. Your uncle may
be here at any moment and if we are not safely

married he can take you away from me again. I will have no way of protecting you. He may even have me arrested for harboring runaway girls since you are both so young. Then I would lose my last chance of saving you. But what's the use of wasting so much time explaining, when you know I love you and am so afraid of losing you! Will you marry me right now Blue Bird?" Fred asked as he took the happy girl in his arms.

Blue Bird laid her weary head on his breast. Words to her were futile. She smiled happily and her dark eyes sparkled brightly as she nodded her head in consent. With her small hand in his, he turned to Red Wing, "Come on sister," he said in a very determined way. "We are not going to let them get away with our little girl again. They may be able to take her away from others but it's against the law to take her away from her husband. That is, if we have such a thing as law out in this country."

In a few minutes, they had awakened the priest and had made their wishes known. He knew Fred very well and liked him, so he wasted no time in performing the ceremony. After this was over, Fred explained in as few words as possible what the trouble was and the young folks went back to Fred's cabin. Fred had his work to do so after a few minutes of visiting he went to work. The two girls settled down to sleep and for the first time since their escape, slept without fear.

That evening Red Wing went home. The first thing Grey Cloud asked her was what had become of Blue

Bird. He became very angry when the girl told him
about her sister. Somehow, he did not blame Red
Wing as much as she had expected him to. He told
her that Blue Bird was only making more trouble
for herself by disobeying him.

Fred and Blue Bird were very happy in their little
cabin and now that they were married, they had no
fear of Nick or the old uncle either. Life seemed to
be everything than one could wish for. Blue Bird
felt so secure now and having always been such a
fearless girl anyway, she did not hesitate to go
anywhere she pleased: to the garrison for groceries,
out gathering flowers and sometimes even fishing
or swimming. It was some time before she ventured
to cross the big river. It was not that she was
afraid. She just did not care to face her uncle. She
felt that he couldn't care to see her either. But one
day Fred was called to see an old man who was sick
and lived up in the hills some distance away. Blue
Bird did up her work, which did not take long, and
then decided to cross the river and visit her mother
and Red Wing who she had not seen for some time.

She climbed into her canoe and started across. Oh,
how good it seemed to be paddling in the water
once more. She always loved the water even if it
had almost caused her death and did cause her to
lose her hearing.

She took her time, paddling lazily and watching in
the water for fish, thinking of Fred and wondering
what he was doing. This was the first time he had
ever been obliged to leave her and he had been very

worried about her. She laughed when she remembered how worried he was when he kissed her good-bye.

Finally, she reached the other shore. Climbing out, she pulled the canoe up on the bank and turned her face toward her old home. She couldn't help but wonder what Fred would think if he knew she was going to see her mother today. She had not thought of it until after Fred left or she would have told him.

Just before she reached the cabin she met Red Wing coming toward her. Instead of looking pleased to see her, Red Wing looked frightened. Rushing towards her, she caught Blue Bird's hand and started leading her back to the river bank and her canoe.

"You mustn't go to the house," she whispered in a frightened tone. "They are waiting for you. Nick is there too, waiting to get you back and Uncle means to get you away from Fred, no matter what. Come with me quick! We don't have a minute to lose!"

But Red Wing didn't take her back to her canoe as she expected but instead led her towards her aunt's house. "We'll stay here for a little while. They don't know you are here yet but Nick is getting ready to go across the river. I'm afraid he will see you. I'm afraid too that he might see your canoe so I'll go and paddle it down river a ways and hide it in the bushes."

After Red Wing had hidden the canoe safe from
prying eyes, she returned to the cabin. She had left
Blue Bird a short distance from their aunt's house.
Although Blue Bird loved her very much and would
have enjoyed seeing her, she was becoming
thoroughly frightened and regretted terribly her
foolishness in venturing so far away from home
alone and decided to hide in the thick bushes not
far from the home of her aunt. Red Wing was soon
there and told her aunt about all that happened.
Their two young cousins were there at the time
and, along with her aunt, they wanted to do all
they could to help Blue Bird. They hated Nick
about as much as she did, for no special reason at
all except for his interest in Blue Bird and they
thought he was just like any other white man and
would cheat on Indians every chance he got. They
were about 18 and 20 years of age so they probably
had traded with Nick more than they cared to
remember.

Quietly slipping away from the others for fear that
Red Wing's presence there would draw suspicion
and cause Nick to come too near, they strolled down
to where they thought they would find Blue Bird.

It would be hard for those who have good hearing
to understand how Blue Bird could tell when
anyone was near, but her sense of feeling
vibrations was more keen than that of other people
and she knew that someone was coming even
though she could neither see nor hear them and she
became very badly frightened in her anxiety,
feeling sure that it must be her enemy Nick Rider.

Suddenly the eager smiling faces of her two cousins appeared through the heavy brush screen and Blue Bird laughed in great relief for she knew that if it were at all possible those two boys would find a way to get her across the river to safety. To her great surprise and chagrin, one of the boys showed her a flask of whiskey, which was protruding from his hip pocket. She hated drinking in the worst way and for one of her cousins to be carrying a flask around was both painful and frightening to her. Seeing that frightened look on the girl's face the young man hasten to explain, but his words only frightened her more.

"See what Nick Rider gave us if we would help him find you! We are going to sell it to some white man for five dollars. We fooled him into believing that we were going to drink it and he thinks we are drunk. He told us to go across the river to see if you were there. He is afraid to go himself. Well, we'll go, but you must go with us. It is dangerous here. Come on! We must hurry! Nick is bad medicine."

Blue Bird sprang to her feet and very quietly the three young people crept through the brush to the river bank where the canoe was hidden. Blue Bird slipped into the canoe while the boys kept watch. They ordered her to lie flat in the bottom of the canoe and then, to her surprise, they threw a blanket over her.

Just as the two boys climbed into the canoe, they heard a shout and looking back they saw Nick coming on the run, his arms waving wildly. "Hey," he yelled. "wait for me. I want to go with you. I think she is over there. Hey wait for me. I say, can't you hear me?"

The boys were well out in the water by now and only paddled the faster and chuckling exultantly, they yelled back sounding very much as though they were not far from being drunk. "No," they yelled. "The canoe is too small and we don't want you in here. You're too fat! We don't want to get drowned! Do you think we're crazy? Maybe you are but we are not!"

They laughed loudly as they plied the paddles faster and faster over the deep fast flowing water until they reached the other shore. The man on the opposite bank stomped his foot angrily. "Why did I give them that bottle anyway?" he grumbled. "I might have known they would get drunk and mess things up for me. Indians are not to be trusted with that stuff. It gets them crazy and now I'll really be in trouble with Grey Cloud! The crazy saps. Now they are too drunk to get the girl, even if they do find her: but if they don't keep their word, it will be the last bottle I'll ever give them."

Then, seeing that the boys had no intentions of coming back after him, he strode angrily back to the cabin where he gave vent to his rage by kicking the dogs and pacing the floor back and forth, drawing many amused glances from Red Wing and her mother and words of sympathy from Owl Eyes.

The old uncle was not at home, but this did not

prevent Nick from making himself at home there, for he still had Owl Eyes on his side. He had his mind made up that he was going to camp there if necessary until the boys brought Blue Bird to him. He knew that sooner or later they would have to come home and time did not mean much to him, when he had so much at stake.

After the boys were certain that Nick had gone back to the cabin, they let Blue Bird get out of the canoe and by dodging through some brush, they managed to get her safely home. Then, borrowing Blue Bird's canoe, they went back across the river and, instead of going straight home, they went to see their aunt. They found Red Wing anxiously waiting for them.

In a few words the boys explained about Blue Bird's narrow escape from Nick and his discomfort in being left behind. They all had a good laugh over it, but Red Wing was still quite worried, not only because of Nick, but because of her uncle as well.

"I worry a lot about my sister," she said. "I wish I could be with her. I'm sure I would feel much better about her. She really should be more careful. She thinks that because she is married no one can bother her, but she doesn't know those people as well as I do. I hear them talking; she can't hear and doesn't know what is going on. Besides, love makes her blind to all the danger around her."

Meanwhile, across the river Blue Bird, after having gone down towards the river to take another look across to see if anyone had pursued her, was walking slowly up the trail towards their cabin. She was picking flowers and taking her time since it appeared to her that the danger was over for the time being. There was no hurry about getting home. It was still early and she had nothing to do for hours. She was greatly disappointed in being defeated in her first attempt to see her mother. She was still a little frightened, but felt a little better now that she was on her own side of the river. The fact that Nick would try to kidnap her now that she was married to someone else seemed so ridiculous that she did not think he would make the attempt again. She was feeling a little lonesome too. Such a brief glimpse of her mother and sister had only been enough to torment her. It had been so long since they had been together.

Suddenly without the slightest warning, a heavy blanket was thrown over her head and she was lifted bodily from her feet and carried in a pair of strong arms. Of course, the first thought was that Nick was holding her. Somehow, he had once more caught up with her and now had her in his power.

She wanted to scream for help but that was impossible for she was scarcely able to breathe. She kicked and struggled with all her might, but it was of no use. The arms that held her seemed to be made of steel. Finally, she felt herself being laid in the bottom of a canoe and she knew that she was being taken back across the river. She wept bitter tears of sorrow and fright. She was afraid that she would never see Fred again, for she knew that if

Nick got her in his clutches once more she would never get back. This brought such bitter agony. She would gladly have welcomed the chance to sink into the river, for looking ahead there seemed to be no peace for her. When they reached the shore, the blanket was removed. To her great relief, she found that her abductor was none other than her old Uncle Grey Cloud. At first, she was too surprised to comprehend just what was happening to her. Then she quickly decided that her uncle was using this method to save her from Nick Rider, but the stern, mean expression on his face caused her much uneasiness. "What did all this mean?" She wondered. "Am I escaping one danger only to find myself in something else and would it all come to the same thing, separated from my beloved husband?"

Her uncle had reasons of his own for abducting his niece. He was a chief, and had forbidden his tribe to marry into the hated white race and here, his own niece had married a white man. Fred was not like most of the white men. Some took their girls and did not bother with the marriage ceremony and after a while or when they had a chance to get a white woman, they left the Indian girl and married one of their own race.

Quite often there were children, nice little children too, but that mattered not at all. If it was a white woman they wanted, well - the Indian woman would have to manage somehow without the white man and this they usually did very well, for that sort of a man, white or otherwise, was worse than no man at all.

That did not interfere with Grey Cloud's plans in the least. He knew that Fred loved Blue Bird and he was sure that the doctor would never leave her for he was not that kind of a man. Fred was not like many of the white men, those who whipped their wives, and Grey Cloud had no complaint there but, regardless of this, he did not like it. He felt that Fred had infringed on his rights and Blue Bird was still his.

She was his before the white doctor ever saw her, or before he had brought her back to life that time. That was fine and he appreciated it very much but he had not given her to him, therefore she still belonged to him to do with as he saw fit. There was nothing to do but steal her back. He had waited a long time for the girls to come home and then they had fooled him by going to Fred first. He knew Blue Bird had been afraid to come home on account of Nick, but she had no business getting married to a white man knowing how he felt about such marriages. He had been very angry with Owl Eyes for selling her sister to the Spaniard, but the meat had tasted good and now that he knew the man had been good to his niece, he harbored no ill feelings towards Nick, but he would see that such a thing did not happen again.

To him it had turned out to be quite a joke in the end and he had enjoyed many a good laugh over it. He meant to keep the unsuspecting man on the watch for Blue Bird as long as he could to keep her whereabouts a secret from him. That would prevent the love-sick Spaniard from searching too far away from home and lessen his chances of discovering how he had been duped.

In the meantime, the two boys who had come so willingly to Blue Bird rescue had reached home, never dreaming that they had unwittingly led their cousin straight into the trap set by their father, a trap that was to prove a greater menace than anything she had ever before encountered.

As they pulled up onto the bank, Nick came running to meet them. "Why didn't you wait for me?" he yelled angrily. "I'll bet I could have found her! You were so full of that fire water, you couldn't see anything! I know she's over there! Red Wing got home and they must have gotten home at the same time so she must be over there!"

"Where's Red Wing now?" the boys asked as they looked around at the deserted cabin.

"She's gone again!" Nick replied disgustedly. "I guess they all went fishing or something. Anyway, she got on her horse and went off with her mother a few minutes ago. Didn't say where they were going, must have been a secret. Say, I'll bet they've gone after Blue Bird while your father is gone so they can clear out with her!"

Then turning swiftly, he ran to where his horse had been turned loose in the corral. When he got there the bars had been let down and the horse was gone

- to the mountains perhaps and it would take days -
maybe weeks to find him. "Who turned my horse
out?" he yelled angrily.

The boys had already started towards their aunt's
cabin and he could hear them laughing, but they
did not answer him, nor even act as though they
had heard him. The boys did not tarry long with
their aunt for it appeared she had some words of
instruction for them and in a very short time they
had caught some ponies and quietly rode away up
the river.

Now there was nothing else to do and no one left to
help him as Owl Eyes had gone with her mother.
He got a rope and started out to find his horse,
determined to go across the river as soon as the
horse was found and find Blue Bird at any cost,
taking her home with him where he was sure Fred
would never find her.

CHAPTER XV   Indian Laws

Blue Bird received a very pleasant surprise when she looked up and saw her mother and Red Wing standing a short distance away beside their horses, as if waiting for her. She ran to her mother and embraced her happily for it had been some time since they had last met. Blue Bird had so sadly missed her mother. It seemed a very long time indeed. In spite of her fright and uneasiness, she was glad to see her loved ones.

Her mother greeted her with tears in her eyes and the smile she bestowed on her little daughter was a very sad one. Red Wing tried to look cheerful, but although she was glad to have her sister with her once more, she would have much rather it had been under far different circumstances.

Blue Bird glanced from one to the other, then to her stern-faced uncle. Her heart sank within her. Somehow Fred seemed a long ways off and she wondered when, if ever, she would see him again. She knew very well her uncle's sentiments about white people and about the Indian laws he had helped to make. He had explained them to her many times.

Since their father had died a few years ago, Grey Cloud had tried to take his place and while they were children he had succeeded very well. He had settled here with his two boys and his adopted family in the friendly little valley not far from

Kettle Falls near the little town called Marcus. They had been quite happy, but as the children grew up, he had found it rather difficult. They had developed a good deal of will power and independence of their own. They were all pretty girls, especially Owl Eyes, who was tall and slender with beautiful dark eyes and long heavy black hair which she wore in two braids down her back. Being the prettiest of the three, besides being gifted with plenty of intelligence which she used to her own special advantage, she grew up to be selfish and overbearing, making life miserable for her two sisters. Red Wing and Blue Bird were both pretty in a quiet way with plenty of determination but with lovely dispositions.

Their uncle loved them all but he was stubborn, always demanding strict obedience in everything. Somehow Owl eyes always managed to keep on the good side of her old uncle even though she was never an obedient girl and seldom obeyed his orders unless to do so would bring some pleasure or benefit to herself. Her two sisters could never figure out how she managed to get away with so much. Owl Eyes was one of the lucky few that could do it. Grey Cloud had been kind to them while they were small but, since they had grown up, he had become selfish and grasping. As was the custom of the Indians, he wanted his girls to marry Indian men who could give him the largest number of ponies or the most money and still have enough to ensure the wives a good living, but above all, they must marry Indian men, not white men. That was one thing he was determined that they should do. It was not altogether selfishness that prompted him to demand this of the girls. He really thought it would be to their advantage to marry men of their own race.

He believed that white men were very unsuitable as husbands for Indian girls. In the first place, he did not think a man could care very much for a girl if he was not willing to pay something for her. In the second place, he did not like them, did not trust them and heartily wished they would all go back to where they came from. An Indian looking for a wife would save until he had enough with which to buy one. A white man, to Grey Cloud's way of thinking, had no sense of value. He seldom paid for his wife and most of them would laugh at you if you demanded payment. This was the funny part of it. The best men were the ones who refused to pay, while men like Nick Rider were more willing to pay and everybody knew he was not a good man. Even men like Nick seldom paid what you asked but would "Jew" you down as far as possible before they would give in. Grey Cloud felt his nieces were far too good for any white man. The ways of the white people were hard to understand.

Blue Bird was pleased that she was given her own gentle pony to ride for she had not ridden him for many days and had missed him so much. She turned to her mother smiling in a way that showed she was trying hard to be brave. "Where are you taking me?" She asked uneasily as they all headed their horses up the river, "and why take me as you would a prisoner? I've done no wrong!"

"We are taking you up the river for a while because we don't trust Nick Rider," her uncle replied convincingly. "He is crazy! We are taking you this way because you would not come with us willingly. You don't know what is best for you and you do very foolish things."

This was partly but not all true and Grey Cloud knew it. He knew that he could not have given her a better answer for Blue Bird was desperately afraid of Nick and there was very little danger of her trying to get away. She would rather die than run the risk of meeting him alone. The girl smiled tearfully at her uncle's explanation but said nothing about this way of escape for her. A menacing glance from her uncle and the fact that he kept a close watch over her every moment of the day quickly discouraged her. She decided that the best she could hope for would be that she would not be gone for more than a few weeks at the most. She knew instinctively that Red Wing had been as much surprised as she was at all the trouble she was in and would have helped her if it had been at all possible.

They traveled for many days, not fast but steadily, always headed towards the north. They stayed as near the river as possible so as to have plenty of water for themselves and the horses. When they camped, they usually got out their fishing tackle and fished.

At such times, Blue Bird might have made an

attempt to escape but she knew that Nick Rider
would be watching for her and would almost be
sure to catch her before she could get to Fred.
There was nothing in the world that she dreaded
worse than that. She made the best of a bad
situation and gave up all ideas of trying to escape.
Besides, her mother and Red Wing had pleaded
with her earnestly not to make any disturbance for
her own sake and theirs too. Terrible things could
happen along the lovely trail, so peaceful and still,
that the rest of the world would never know of it.
Terrible things had happened many times and
many more would happen in such lovely places
where feelings ran as high as they were in this
small cavalcade: feelings of fear, hate and
desperation.

Nevertheless, Blue Bird being young and full of
vitality realized that if this trip had been taken
under different circumstances, she would have
enjoyed it very much. As it was, she found some
comfort in knowing she was getting farther and
farther away from Nick Rider. It gave her no small
amount of pleasure to know that while he was
spending his days looking for her and his nights
watching the trails for their return, she was
putting many miles between them.

The Columbia River scenery is always beautiful.
The rock-bound river itself, wide, swift and deep,
rolling over its rocky bed was sometimes a mighty
roaring thing, seeming almost alive in its mad rush
to the ocean. At other times, still majestic but
serene and peaceful, it lapped its banks with a

cooling sound.

The high mountains covered with great trees and thick underbrush were decorated here and there with beautiful wild Tiger Lilies and other mountain flowers.

Occasionally, they would cross a small stream hurrying to meet the Columbia River, filling the air with its rippling music, furnishing, for all who wished to stop and partake, a good cool drink of delicious water straight from the mountain springs from which it was supplied.

The mountains were full of wild game and Grey Cloud was an expert hunter. The family was never without meat. Huckleberries grew abundantly here, as well as other mountain berries, so they were well supplied with fruit.

How many days it took to make the journey is not known but finally they reached a small log cabin away up in British Columbia beside the beautiful Arrow Lakes. There Grey Cloud decided to make their home for the coming months. This was his old camping grounds and he knew there would be plenty of fur bearing animals, enough to keep him busy for a long time.

They spent the winter here, with good results, then in the spring they journeyed still farther north to the banks of the upper Arrow Lakes where they remained for some time. Traveling back and forth from the upper lakes to the lower lakes and back

again, they hunted and trapped for four years.
They had accumulated hundreds of pelts which
Grey Cloud well knew should be worth a great deal
of money. He was an Indian, although wiser than
most Indians of his tribe. He still did not know how
to go about getting anywhere near what his furs
were worth. He knew that eventually he would sell
them to some white man for whatever he could
induce him to pay for them. He knew it would be
far below what they were worth.

In the meantime, Fred was kept busy. He had
reluctantly given up the search for Blue Bird.
There was much to be done in this glorious land of
the West and few who really knew how to do it. He
was never idle for there were many things that he
was capable of doing besides being the only doctor.

For one thing, there was not much that he did not
know about boats. He went to Portland and helped
to build a steamship that was later to steam all the
way up the Columbia River to the Arrow Lakes. It
was a glorious undertaking but often quite
hazardous. Where the water was deep and not too
rough, they made good time enjoying the
satisfaction that any great achievement brings to
those who promote it. It was not all pleasure. They
often had trouble getting over the worst rapids.
They were obliged to use guy ropes and pulleys to
get over some of the worst places. They would
fasten the pulleys to some solid trees or rocks on
shore. With the help given by the power of the boat
itself, they would pull on the ropes attached to the
pulleys, gradually working it upstream. After much

hard work, sweat and discouragement they would
finally reach smoother waters and taste the joy
once more of victory.

Fred was every bit a navigator as he had been in
his boyhood days when he first went to sea. He was
never so happy as when he was working on the
steamboat; especially when cruising up the
Columbia River, and the harder the work proved to
be, the better he liked it. It made his worries about
Blue Bird easier to bear. It was dangerous work for
never before had a steamboat ventured so far up
the Columbia River. They never knew when they
might get caught on some unusable island or rock
pile where a boat could be ground to pieces in no
time at all.

At Northport, they experienced their worst
troubles. Without it being in the late spring time,
when the river was at its highest and the water the
deepest, it would have been impossible to have
gotten the boat up at all. It took a number of days
to get the boat past the rapids with a great deal of
hard work and the steady use of guy ropes and
pulleys.

Finally, they reached deeper water and less big
boulders protruding out or too near the surface of
the water. The great boat was gliding along
beautifully. It was with much rejoicing that they
finally reached the lower Arrow Lakes with the
boat for the first time. It was the opening of
another great industry in the Northwest.

Some of the men on the boat were fur traders and
did a good business up there in the North, after
they once reached their destination. It was
worthwhile in itself of all the trouble it had cost
them to get there, for there was much to be gained
and getting the boat back down to Marcus would be
easy. This would not be before they had traded
their grocery goods, pretty glass beads, tobacco and
other sorts of merchandise for enough furs to make
a cargo. They would then steam on back down to
Marcus. Here the furs would be loaded onto Pack
horses and would begin the long hard journey down
to the Dalles, Oregon. They would cross the
Spokane River about 30 miles above where it
empties into the Columbia River. The Spokane
River was not very deep here. It was hard to ford it
during the winter and summer months. It was
impossible to cross that way during the spring
time, owing to the high water caused by melting
snow.

It took a good many horses to carry all the furs. To
successfully get them across the river without
losing any or without letting any of them get down
into the deep water where they would get wet and
cause a delay in their long journey was quite an
accomplishment.

As the boat sailed through the lower Arrow Lake,
Fred stood and watched the Indian camps along the
banks of the lake and wondered about them. What
kind of people they were, how they looked and
dressed, what language they spoke, etc. never
dreaming that Blue Bird stood there in the brush

watching the wonderful steamboat as it glided smoothly by.

If only he had gone to that camp for furs what a difference it would have made to him and the one he was most concerned about.

Blue Bird's thoughts were taking her back to Marcus where she knew the boat must have passed a few days before. She would never have guessed that Fred had helped build the boat. "I know that Fred must be very anxious about me," she thought. "I only wish I could find a way to get on that boat. If only they would stop here! I know I could get on. I could make them understand that I am Fred's wife and I want to go home. I know they would let me go with them." But the boat sailed right on by without stopping.

If she could have known that, at that very time, Fred was standing on the boat unknowingly watching her uncle's camp and wondering about her, she would have been desperate to find a way and would have tried in some way to reach him. He would not allow himself to think of the stubborn obsession that might be in the breast of the old Indian: that the white man was a grasping, overbearing, murdering invader and that Grey Cloud must not let his children fall under the white man's power.

Blue Bird knew that if she tried real hard she could find her way home if she did not get caught, which she probably would. If she managed to escape them, she would very likely starve to death before she could reach Marcus. They were many long miles from there and besides there was Nick Rider still to be feared. So, she dared not make the break that would be so sure to end up in failure and would eventually end up in more trouble for her and her loved ones.

One day her uncle came to her. "Blue Bird," he said as he stood with folded arms, his wrinkled old face set in the stern lines that Blue Bird had learned to dread so terribly. "You are a grown woman now and you should marry some good young brave and have a home of your own."

 Blue Bird was horrified at these words. She knew that the white man's marriage meant nothing to him but to her, her marriage to Fred meant everything. She shook her head sadly, the ever-ready tears sprang to her eyes. "I am sorry Uncle but I cannot do is you say!"

"I know why!" Her uncle answered angrily. It is because of that white man who wanted you, but not enough to pay me anything for you! He is just like the rest of the white men, only he is one of the worst. He wants what is our greatest possession, our own flesh and blood, for nothing. He doesn't even offer to pay as much as Nick Rider does, and Nick is not a good man."

"But Fred loves me and I love him!" The girl protested.

"Loves you!" her old uncle jeered. "How can he love you when you are worth nothing to him? Do you think it is love that makes him want to take away the thing we prize more than anything else in the world, without even asking for it? If that is white man's love then I think it is all wrong. If you go to him you will be cheating your mother and uncle, we who have fed and clothed you all these years. You would repay our kindness to you in disobedience. You would spoil our chances of ever getting anything for all the years we have spent in bringing you up, and you would find your punishment. You would find that he is nothing but a cheat, that he is not a good man and that he only wants you by his side while you are young and beautiful! You will find that he will not marry you and when he sees a white woman he will do as many white men do. He will leave you for her."

At this Blue Bird could control herself no longer. Springing to her feet she faced her uncle with hands clenched and eyes blazing. "I've been afraid to tell you everything! I've been afraid of you, my Uncle, but now I must tell you. I must convince you that he does love me. You must not speak so!" she cried, "because he is my husband! We were married by the priest just a short time before you brought me here, and now that I have told you, what's going to happen to me? I'm afraid for my life and I'm tired," she sobbed brokenheartedly.

The old man stood there glaring at her as if frozen to the ground, too badly stunned by the news to believe his ears. "Married!" He finally gasped. "You

married to that man? You dare to turn against me,
your own uncle, for him? You'll never see him
again! That's a white man's marriage. Nothing,
nothing, I tell you nothing!" He raised his fist as if
to strike her. The frightened girl cringed away from
him. Instead of striking her the old man appeared
to be thinking deeply. He folded his arms and stood
eyeing his little niece speculatively as she stood
before him, a picture of despair. "In this wilderness,
so many miles from our home country, you can
forget that you are, what you call married! You no
longer belong to that man. He stole you away from
me, as all of his race have stolen from Indians, but
I have taken you back. You belong to me now!!
Young Wolf wants to marry you. You will accept
him. He is our kind and his father is rich. He will
give me many ponies for you."

The girl covered her face with her trembling hands.
"No, no, "she wailed, "not Young Wolf. I hate him!"

"That makes no difference. You shall do as I say. It
is your duty to obey your elders!" was the stern
reply. With that he turned and walked away.

Blue Bird stood as if paralyzed, the words of her
uncle ringing in her ears. Marry Young Wolf! No!
No! Never! She would die first. No one, not even
her own mother and her uncle together, could force
her to marry that man. She hated him. She sank to
the damp ground, her heart torn with pain. Oh
Fred! Fred!" she mourned pitifully. "Why do you
not come and get me? I'll die here. How can I bear
it?"

She let her despairing eyes wander over the lake to the great boat sailing over the peaceful water, so still, so beautiful and so gloriously pale. She wished with all her heart that she were on it and that in some way she might escape this terrible danger. The boat was growing smaller and smaller in the distance until finally it became only a small speck.

Fred, if you could only have heard the pitiful voice of your lost bride!

CHAPTER XVI   Loyalty

Blue Bird soon decided that Grey Cloud was very much in earnest about Young Wolf, for he never let her forget for a single moment what the young man's intentions were. He encouraged the fellow in every way possible to spend all the time he wished at his camp.

The girl grew to hate his shuffling, stealthy footsteps as he came near her. She hated worse still, if that were possible, the gleam that would come to his small black eyes whenever their eyes met, which was very seldom and never voluntarily, for Blue Bird never looked in his direction purposely. She was not completely discouraged until she found that her uncle had enlisted the help of her mother. This destroyed entirely her faith in human justice for she had depended so much on the help of her mother and now she was helping those who were bent on ruining her body and soul.

For the first time in her life she was really afraid of her own relatives. First it was Owl Eyes, then her uncle and now her own dear mother who had turned traitor. Red Wing was the only one who would still be glad to help her and she did not have a chance in the world.

Grey Cloud was becoming more disagreeable every day. Instead of being the kind understanding uncle that he had been all the years that Blue Bird was small. Her refusal to obey his unreasonable demands was causing him to become more cruel and formidable every day, until Blue Bird was becoming desperate. She had taken about all the abuse that she could stand, but still refused to do his bidding. He had first tried pleading with her, then scolding. Then he had tried whipping her, but all to no avail.

Finally, the old man decided to hold a council and, getting the Indians together in the country, he put the question to them. After much airing of opinions, arguing and questioning of those concerned, they all agreed that it was her duty to marry the man of her uncle's choice. Young Wolf was the son of a chief and they considered it a disgrace for a girl to refuse their chief's son in marriage. This, they thought, should be considered a great honor, and for one of their daughters to refuse it because of her preference for a white man was outrageous and not to be tolerated at all. Blue Bird steadily refused to listen, and clung constantly to her own conclusions the things that Fred taught her. She still hoped, although at times her hopes were very discouraging, that the time might come when she would be with Fred once more. She knew that if that time ever came, she would be glad that she had remained true, no matter what it cost, and that nothing could ever separate them again even if she was obliged to go with her husband wherever and whenever he went for the rest of their lives.

Needless to say, when Blue Bird flatly refused to listen to the judges, Grey Cloud was very angry. He was not only angry, he was raging mad and for a moment there, before all of the people, she was almost afraid for her life. Her mother was between two fires. She loved her little daughter very much and had stood about all she could stand but was obliged to agree with her brother that Blue Bird by order of the council should obey her uncle.

After the council meeting, Grey Cloud was worse than ever before. He was after Blue Bird continually, trying in every way to break her spirit until Falling Leaf thought she would go mad. She might have found some way to help her daughter, but she lacked the courage. In spite of her love for Blue Bird, her narrow and weak mind could only see one side of the question. No matter what reasons the girl may have, there was only one way out. She must obey her uncle and the council members or take her punishment. "Blue Bird, my poor girl!" she said one day after her uncle had given her an unmerciful beating, "Why don't you do as your uncle says? He will kill you if you don't do as he says."

"I don't care if he does," the weeping girl replied. "I'll never marry that horrid man! Uncle can kill me if he wants to. I'd rather be dead than married to Young Wolf. That is a good name for him and I hate him! I'd rather die, only I wish he would hurry up and get it over with."

Finally, Grey Cloud decided that whipping would never bring about the results that he desired for Blue Bird who, true to her word, would rather die than give up. He hit upon the idea of starving her into submission. He bound her hand and foot with strong strips of rawhide and left her to starve for a while, forbidding the others under threat of severe punishment to give her food or water without his permission. The rawhide was tied so tightly that the strips around her wrists cut deeply into the flesh, causing her untold misery all that day as she lay in the hot suffocating teepee. At night, she was in the same condition, only it was a little cooler. She could not sleep and her wrists and ankles pained her so badly that she began to think that her uncle must surely mean to let her die this way, and although she was still young and had a lot to live for, she would have welcomed death if she was to find relief in no other way.

On the second night, Red Wing could bear it no longer. The thought of her beloved sister, there in the teepee suffering and alone, was too much for her to stand any longer. After the others had gone to bed and were asleep, she slipped out of bed and very quietly crept out and into the teepee where her sister lay wide awake, sick in body and soul. The two girls cried when they saw each other and Red Wing immediately began loosening the tight bands around her poor sister's wrists and ankles. She had brought some water for which Blue Bird was very grateful Indeed, and a little food which had been part of Red Wing's supper. Blue Bird was too sick at heart to be hungry, but was thankful that her sister had gone to so much trouble and had taken such risks to bring her. The water was so good and she drank every bit of it with a promise from her sister that she would bring her another drink before morning. Red Wing knew that she dare not remain with her sister more than a few minutes for her uncle might miss her and she knew that if she got caught she may never again be able to help her sister. So, as soon as Blue Bird had disposed of every bit of the food, for she had decided that she was hungry after all, and drank the last of the water, Red Wing gently fastened the cruel thongs back onto her sister's wrist and ankles, only not as tight as they were before and in a way that would prevent their cruel uncle from knowing that they have been tampered with. This kept up for about two weeks. Every day her mother or Grey Cloud would come in and ask her the same question.

Blue Bird continued to give them the same answer. "No." She would say. "I'll never marry anyone for I'm married to Fred!"

Her mother and Red Wing were almost desperate for the girl's life and Her mother took to sneaking a little food and water to her also, never guessing Red Wing was doing the same thing. Between the two, Blue Bird managed to keep alive.

One day Grey Cloud came to the conclusion that his efforts were worse than useless, and if he persisted in torturing his niece so severely, she would lose all her beauty and then he would not be able to get any ponies at all for her. So, he let her go free, but refused to allow her to eat at the table with the rest of the family. She was abused in ways that were almost as bad as the former punishment had been. In fact, by her uncle and by the others, she was scarcely treated like a human being at all. He treated her no better than he did his dogs and would tolerate no show of kindness towards her. Blue Bird would look at him in wonder.

"How can one human be so cruel to another?" she would muse as she gazed at him sadly. "I can scarcely believe he is really my uncle, the one I used to love so dearly. He seems to be some horrible stranger and my mother, she is so weak, I really believe she would let him kill me before she would risk facing his wrath over me. She is so afraid of him, but I don't blame her too much for it. She has always obeyed him because he has taken care of us. He is a very cruel master, even if he is her brother."

It was now a little over four years since they had come to British Columbia and Grey Cloud was beginning to think of home. He had done enough trapping for a while. He had enough pelts to load his horses down, and he was tired of trapping. Also, Young Wolf had given up in disgust, concluding that he would rather marry someone who did not require so much persuading. There was nothing to keep them here any longer. Grey Cloud was still determined to force Blue Bird to give up her relations with Fred, so he kept her under close guard all the time. She was not allowed her meals, but generally she was too heartsick to care whether she ate or not. Then as they reached the good old U.S. and she realized that they were really headed towards home once more, she began to feel the thrill that everyone feels when returning home after being away for such a long time. Deep in her heart, untouched by the terrible punishment and black despair she had experienced, there still lay a faint spark of hope that she might find Fred at the end of the trail, while her uncle, who was still very angry with her and refused to allow her to eat with them, merely tossed her a few scraps of food such as he gave to the hungry dogs, as she sat on a log or rock apart from the rest of the family. The little spirit of hope grew stronger. What was there left for her, except her determination, which was growing by the hour as the hours sped by, to go to Fred or die in the attempt.

No one cared what happened to her except Red Wing and possibly her mother. There was no one else to care if she got killed in her break for liberty. So, the faint hope grew into a real live spark. She would risk it all to find Fred or a grave, where at least there would be peace and rest. There were things to endure here on earth that were much worse to endure than death to the body. The old priest had taught her to believe in God and she never failed to say her rosary every night and often at other times when she had a chance.

They had not brought their ponies. Grey cloud had decided that they had plenty of them at home, so they made themselves canoes, which they loaded with the pelts and supplies. They started down the river early one morning after turning the ponies loose on the range to shift for themselves. Grey Cloud's main objective in going back to the garrison was to get some groceries for the coming winter and, as that time was not very far off, he had decided that to go by canoe would be the speediest way. He figured that the ponies at home would carry them all back to the lakes again for another winter's trapping. It was lovely paddling down the great river, especially in the evenings or early mornings. If all had been well with Blue Bird she would have enjoyed the trip completely, but in spite of all her troubles she did gain some peace and happiness from the steady splashing of the cool water and the soft breeze which fanned her aching brow. Although being young and naturally a healthy girl, she dreamed and her dream gave her hope.

It did not take them nearly as long to travel down the river as it had going up. The trip was much more restful for all. They were getting along really well and making good time until someone noticed that his canoe was springing a small leak. They were just opposite the town of Bossburg and still had some distance to go. They decided to look over all the canoes for weak places. They hauled the canoes all up on the bank and went to work on them. They first unloaded the canoes, then turned them all bottom side up. Satisfying themselves that they all needed repairing, they proceeded to tear the bark from the canoes. This had to be done first thing in order to make a good strong foundation for the new pieces of bark. Hot pitch was then poured onto the clean places to be mended and the new pieces carefully laid on and pressed firmly down. In a few hours, the canoe was as good as new. This was a tedious job and took much time and work. It took more time than Grey Cloud cared to take. It

was getting late in the season and he was getting in
a hurry to buy his groceries and whatever was
needed so that they could get back into the
mountains before winter overtook them. Red Wing,
Owl Eyes and their mother were out gathering
pitch, a hard and tiresome job.

To keep Blue Bird from getting any ideas in her
head now that they were so near home, she was
told to stay at camp and look after supper. The
garrison where Fred lived was not many miles
away and Grey Cloud was afraid to trust her out of
his sight. Besides that, he did not trust Red Wing
or her mother too much either. It was safer to keep
her where he could keep an eye on her himself.

Blue Bird busied herself around camp for a while,
finding plenty to do, until she finally found that she
was short of water. Taking two water bags made of
bark, she started down to the river bank passing
her uncle and two young cousins on the way. They
were all working on the canoes.

One of the boys smiled at her as she went by never
ceasing to work for an instant. Blue Bird saw that
he was still very busy pulling old patches off the
canoe he was working on. She was walking slowly.
Her uncle and the other boy were so busy that they
did not look up as they made preparations for
pouring on the hot pitch.

So intent were they in making every patch fit just
right and in seeing that the pitch was heated to
just the right temperature, Blue Bird knew that for

the moment she was entirely forgotten. "What a chance," she thought, her heart beating suffocatingly. When she reached the edge of the river, she quietly walked out into the water. No one noticed her. It was nothing unusual for one to go out into the deep water to get a good fresh drink of water or to wash their faces. No one paid any attention to her. She did not stop there! All thoughts of danger had fled from her mind. She was like a wild animal in sight of freedom. The river was wide and at any moment her uncle might see her and take out after her, or worse yet, send her two young cousins who dared not openly disobey their father. If she did escape there was still Nick to contend with. As she quietly walked along, her feet slipping and sliding on the slippery rocks, these thoughts all tormented her a little. She did not stop walking, neither did she glance back nor hasten her step. She thought that the cousin who had smiled at her must have guessed by this time what was in her mind. She trusted both of the boys not to give her away as long as her secret would not bring harm to them.

A meeting with Nick would be tragic but why think of that now? Then there was the danger of drowning! She had once almost drowned and remembered the time and sensation very well. Drowning was far better than living with her uncle with the prospects of going back to the mountains for another winter. It only took a few short moments until she had walked out into the deep water where it was beginning to be quite swift. She ventured a backward glance.

Apparently, no one except the one cousin had seen her. Hastily now she walked into deeper water, deep enough to come over her head. Just as she reached water that would cover her from sight, she reached down and picked up a large rock which she placed on her head. She had dropped the water bags which went floating down the river. She made not a sound now or extra ripples on the water as she walked along the bottom of the mighty river, the friendly waters covering up her tracks as well. She walked swiftly, never missing a step, never stumbling nor falling, as she stepped on the slippery rocks until she could hold her breath no longer. She dropped the heavy stone and rose to the surface. She glanced back once more as she started swimming madly for the other shore. Apparently, no one had noticed her disappearance. She was many yards away from the shore. She had almost reached the middle of the river when a roar of rage sounded over the still waters. She knew with a jubilant feeling in her heart that at last she had been discovered but that it was too late. Her old uncle would not dare to come out after her and her two loyal cousins would not even if they could. They feared their father, but not to the extent of swimming the Columbia River for him, especially when there was nothing in the world they would rather see than for her to escape from her tyrannical old uncle.

She was an excellent swimmer with a strong steady stroke so it was not long until she had reached the other shore. She glanced back at the men and imagined that she could see a grin of satisfaction on the swarthy faces of her cousins as they hurriedly turned and started working on their canoes again, so that they could cross the river after her. They knew very well that they could never catch their little cousin now that she had so cleverly escaped her uncle's clutches.

As Blue Bird hurried down the trail a short distance from the river, she felt the thud of a horse's hooves beating on the ground not far away. She knew that someone must be coming down the same trail on which she was traveling. Instantly her thoughts turned to Nick Rider. She quickly hid in the bushes. She could not bear the thought of meeting Nick Rider! Not now, after all she had been through and so near home too.

As the rider came near, she peeked out to see who it might be. To her great joy and surprise, she saw that it was one of her old friends, Eliza Penkston. With her buckskin dress still dripping wet, Blue Bird stepped out from the shelter of the bushes and spoke. Eliza was very much surprised, naturally but, having heard something of Blue Bird's story, she instantly guessed that there was no time to lose. She took the shivering girl up behind her on the horse, wet clothes and all, and rode swiftly on down the road.

As they rode along, Blue Bird told her in sketches of her terrible experiences. Of course, Eliza was really shocked and very angry with all who had participated in the torture of her young friend. She knew that Blue Bird must have been wildly desperate and filled with the fear of death to have dared to swim the mighty river. Swimming the Columbia River was no job for anyone but an expert swimmer. Eliza had known for many years that Grey Cloud was a very cruel man and that he hated white people worse than poison. She never thought that he could ever be so mean as to take it out on his little niece.

When she voiced her horror at all the things he had done, she was surprised at the response Blue Bird gave.

"I don't blame my uncle so much," she said sadly. "After all it was the white people who gave my father the fire water which was the real cause of my father's death. Because of that and many other reasons, my uncle thinks I should hate the white people as much as he does. I can't hate people who are good to me, and for me especially, when I love Fred and wouldn't turn against him for anything in the world."

Eliza smiled and wondered how anyone so closely related to Grey Cloud with all his unforgiving cruelty and manners could be so tender hearted and forgiving. She shook her head for she knew that if she had been in Blue Bird's place she could never have done it.

CHAPTER XVII   At The Garrison

Life at the garrison was never at a standstill. Most of the men were out in the wild West for what the country had to offer them in trade. They were anxious to be friends with the Indians and were not hunting trouble with them, some because they really liked the Indians and others because they were afraid of them, still others because they knew that any trouble with the Indians would spoil their business dealings with them. As a rule, the white people were always willing to help the Indians whenever an opportunity presented itself, especially in teaching the ways of their own civilization including Christianity.

For the Indians, like most humans, must have something super-human to worship, some power greater than human to call on in time of need. Before the missionaries and priests came and taught them that they must worship the Almighty God, they believed in the great spirit. The great spirit was not a god made by hands but he was the spirit father of all the spirits. The Indians believed that a certain animal, plant or anything that grows had a spirit which was the guiding light or helper of some human being. This helper, as it was called, was a very important figure in the lives of the people. The young Indians were taught by their elders to believe that the main object in any boy's or girl's life was to seek until they found their own particular helper. (This was to be done at about the age of 14.) Thus, the boy or girl was obliged to climb to the top of the highest mountain in sight and spend the night alone regardless of animals or anything else that might be enough to frighten the daylights out of them. It was something that must not be neglected or postponed until some more opportune time. It was in their line of duty and must be attended to at the proper time of life.

The first thing they saw in the morning with life in it, whether a deer, bear, other animal, tree or a plant, was their own personal helper. It was the spirit of the animal or living thing that they had to call on in times of trouble or when needing help of any kind. In other words, this was his or her god for the rest of their lives. The priests had very little difficulty in gaining a foothold among the Indians. The main thing was to gain their confidence. In every tribe, it was always possible to get at least a few of the Indians to trust the priests. They reasoned that these white people with long black robes were not trying to gain possession of their land nor were they even interested in their beloved hunting grounds. All they wanted from the Indians was their confidence and something for their church. Sometimes the donations requested was enough to make the Indian wonder what the great spirit did with so much money. Most of the priests were honest men and asked for only what the people wished to donate to the good cause. Since some of them had always worshiped their own great spirit, it was not so hard to get many of them to turn from their way of worship and take up the white man's way. The young people, who sometimes found it hard work, discouraging and often frightening to find their own helper, were especially glad to listen to the priest.

The priests explained to them that it was all unnecessary to go to such lengths to find a better, much better helper. In time, many of the old people learned to accept the white man's God, the priests finding it much easier for them to shift from one great spirit to the right one, than if they had been idol worshipers. The idol is made of solid material and is visible to the eye. There were some of the Indians, like Grey Cloud, who cared nothing for the white people or their ways and would much prefer to be left entirely alone to do whatever they pleased and to worship as they pleased, but the majority of the young Indians around Marcus and the surrounding country liked the white people very much. They liked the way they lived and the kind of clothes they wore. They could see great advantage in learning to read and write.

The school that Fred had started had grown considerably in the past four years since Blue Bird had disappeared. Of course, Fred did not draw a salary but the people who were interested in the work gave him whatever they could afford, which was not very much. This did not hinder Fred from building the school from a small school held in his own log cabin to a large enough group of school children to afford a real school house built of logs and a hired teacher. This gave Fred the freedom he needed for his other work. Fred was feeling quite discouraged during all the time that Blue Bird had been gone. He had never received a single word from or about her. He was beginning to wonder if she were still alive. He had heard that the family was somewhere in the mountains hunting but he had no idea about what part of the country they were in. He often wondered why Blue Bird, if she was still in the land of the living, did not send him some word if only to let him know how she was. He thought it would relieve his terrible suspense. At times, like a thief, a thought would creep into his tortured mind. "What if she had found someone else?" but he would quickly banish the wicked thought. He knew no matter what happened or where she was, he had enough confidence in her to feel that she would always be true to him. He knew that Nick Rider had left the country about the same time as Blue Bird did. This did not trouble him, as Blue Bird would not have her old enemy to contend with. How was she to know this? Fred felt as though he was going around in circles and getting nowhere fast. The sorrow of losing Blue Bird and not knowing her whereabouts was driving him out of his mind.

One day he sat looking out through the window. He been thinking a lot about Blue Bird today. All sorts of thoughts and even unwelcome suspicions kept flitting through his mind. He wondered if he might be foolish to be still worrying about her. Perhaps she was married again by now to someone of her own race. It was not impossible under the circumstances. Deep in his heart he knew better and was glad for he could not bear the thought of Blue Bird loving anyone else. He finally decided to go visit the old priest who lived at the garrison and was a very good friend of his. Here he was sure to learn the latest news from the East. Of course, the news was not very new by the time it had crossed the continent from east to west. There was nothing in the world that could travel any faster than a horse or other animal. It would take many weeks for a horse to travel across the plains and over the mountains to Marcus.

Fred, whose head was always full of visions, remarked at times when wishing for news that someday people would be able to step off a balcony into a vehicle and sail away through the air, but thoughts such as these were not much help at that time.

When Fred reached the Garrison, he was handed a letter from his mother. He had written to her some time ago and in it he had told her of his love for Blue Bird and had been expecting an answer. Taking the letter, he quickly tore it open. He had no idea what to expect but hoped for the best. He glanced over the pages, first to see if they were all alive and well and if the Civil War was still causing them any trouble. The letter made him very happy. As he went on reading his face grew white and the lines on his face set and stern. His mother, his own mother who he had loved so dearly and had thought loved him, had denounced him as a traitor to his family and to his country by lowering himself to the level of an Indian girl.

"Well," he thought as he thrust the letter into his pocket, "that's settled! I'm not really surprised.

Indians are nothing but savages to those who have never been west of the Great Lakes. I don't blame mother a bit. She could not be expected to understand, but after all, she was doing a lot of worrying for nothing. Poor mother! I only wish she could have known Blue Bird."

He went to see the old priest who was always glad to welcome him to his cabin. They were both interested in the same line of work, that of educating the Indians. The two had a great deal in common. The priest shook his hand warmly and led him to the most comfortable chair in the cabin.

"I'm so glad to see you," he said smiling jovially. "You are a very busy man. I get to see so little of you."

"Yes," Fred answered. "There has been a lot of sickness around here which has kept me pretty busy most of the time. If I had time to think of old age, I could very easily make up my mind that I was getting old, but I have no time for such morbid thoughts. There is a lot of work around here to do and not many of us to do it."

The old priest nodded his head gravely, "Yes, there is a lot of work, too much, with very few real workers. So many of our white men are here working only for personal benefit. They have no time nor thought for the Indians. Some of them are our best citizens. They are plenty busy attending strictly to their own business of making a real stake out here. Many of those who go out of their way to be friendly to the Indians do so only to get a better chance to beat or cheat the Indians out of their valuable furs or whatever they have. The Indians never know the real value of anything. It would be easy to beat them out of a fortune. Only today an Indian brought a huge pile of furs which should have brought him a very high price and laid them on the stone floor. He was very proud of his great wealth. It represented many months of hard and successful work. With a grunt of satisfaction, he wrapped his full-length blanket around his long form and stalked up and down the floor, back and forth, up and down, while the white men gathered there looked on in amused curiosity, until his rolling eyes rested on what he apparently had been looking for. It was a huge butcher knife worth about one dollar and a half. Picking it up gravely he thrust it into his belt and walked out of the store with the satisfied air of a man who had just turned in the results of a whole year's work and had received full value for it. Another time an Indian saw a gun in the store that he wanted and wanted badly. The storekeeper held the gun in front of him, lengthwise with one end on the floor, telling the Indian if he got him enough pelts piled flat to reach the full length of the gun the Indian could have the gun. The Indian nodded and went out and climbed onto his horse and rode away. Many months passed by and one day the Indian returned. His ponies were loaded down with furs. In a very business-like way, he removed them from the backs of his ponies, carried them into the store and piled them onto the floor until he had a pile almost as high as he was tall. Very gravely he walked over, taking the gun

and held it up beside the furs. Nodding to the
storekeeper he went out, climbed onto his pony, the
other ponies falling behind, and disappeared
towards his teepee proudly bearing his new gun,
the results of much time and hard work. To these
Indians both these trades were fair enough but to
us, well, we know better."

Fred shook his head sadly. "Yes, we know better.
Nothing truer was ever said. We know too that,
although we pose as good honest citizens, some of
us are only pirates. Pirates on land. For the life of
me I can't see where we are any better than the
pirates on the high seas. The pirates at sea take
what doesn't belong to them. So do we! They kill to
get it. So do we! The only difference I can see is
that they don't pretend to be friends but we do."

"That's it, exactly!" the old priest agreed, but of
course that doesn't mean that we should not buy
their furs or whatever they have to sell. Those who
buy could well afford to give them a good profit and
still make money for themselves. It seems that the
first white men that came to this country were as a
rule pretty decent, but of late years, many who
come out here are not so good. They cheat more.
They bring whiskey and gamble with the Indians.
This enables them to get about anything they want
from the Indians for practically nothing. Instead of
teaching them to be good citizens, they teach them
to drink and gamble. They get them drunk, beat
them out of everything they own, kick them out and
send them home, if they still have a home to go to,
where they, crazy with drink, fight and beat up

their families and kill both Indians and white people alike!"

"It's too bad," Fred replied. "Some came out West to help the Indians and others that followed them tear down all the good that has been done. It only goes to prove that those of us who really wish to help the Indians must work that much harder and faster to beat the others at their own game!"

"That's the spirit!" the priest exclaimed. "Work and lots of it is what we need and the time may yet come when the Indians will see good in our presence and know that some of us, at least, are here for their own good: to teach them the needs of their spiritual life and an all-around better life. There is no doubt that the Indians need civilization as a majority. Some of them are heartless and cruel. They are not more so than many of the white people. Take the experience of last year for instance. An Indian boy went into a store up the river one day. Seeing a pair of boots he desired to own, he sat down and very calmly put them on his feet. They fit him perfectly, so why not keep them? Without a word of explanation to the proprietor, he walked out doors. The storekeeper, seeing what his intentions were, followed him out and hastened to stop him. "Take off the boots!" he yelled angrily. Instead of stopping, the frightened boy tried to make his getaway but was caught and forced to remove the coveted boots. Very much insulted, he rode away. In about an hour, he reappeared on the opposite bank of the river. The store was situated as near the edge of the river as possible and the river was narrow there. The Indian boy had a good gun and was soon very busy taking pot shots at the store and anyone who dared to show his face. Of course, there was a wild scramble for shelter. Almost immediately the storekeeper managed to send word to the nearest fort for help. In double quick time the soldiers were there and eager to start shooting at every Indian in sight. This was uncalled for since only one Indian was responsible for it all. The Indians scampered everywhere for shelter. Being so taken by surprise, they were unprepared for the onslaught and many of them were killed outright. Was that fair? No, very definitely it was not fair. The soldiers, and other men who took part, took advantage of their privilege as soldiers and deliberately murdered the helpless Indians in cold blood, and yet they say the Indians are cruel and heartless. Maybe they are, but who is responsible for most of their cruelty? Not they, for whatever they do, they do in ignorance or in self-defense. It is us, the whites, who work deliberately and intelligently, if I may dare to use the words describing our actions, with our training and education to show us how to do the most damage or good whatever the object may be. We know exactly what we are doing and why. The Indian does not. There my friend is the difference."

"Yes, you are right," Fred replied, "and that is only one example out of many that have never been mentioned. In fact, most white people would much rather these things could be forgotten, unless you can remember to think of them from the white man's point of view. For instance, a case such as

the one I knew to happen right here in Marcus was
so outrageous that it makes my blood boil every
time I think of it. An Indian woman and her 14-
year-old daughter went into a store. The woman
became interested in some goods. While she was
examining them, the white man who owned the
store, drew the young girl into a small store room
and closed the heavy door. The mother glancing up
to ask the man something about the goods was
surprised to find that her little daughter had
disappeared. Just then she heard the girl scream
for help. The woman immediately became
frightened and rushed to the door but found it was
locked. Frantically she tore around trying to find an
entrance to the store room. She could hear her little
daughter pleading to her. She finally crawled
through a window, and seizing a large butcher
knife, stabbed the man before he could think of a
way to defend himself. He died almost immediately,
probably not even realizing that the wages of sin is
death. The poor woman, who according to the law
was not guilty, sneaked out the back door and,
taking her daughter, hurried home as fast as she
could. Gathering up a few necessary items of
clothing and food, she escaped to the mountains.
The white people, finding the man stabbed to
death, sent out a search party and ran her down
before she could find a good hiding place. They took
her back to headquarters. Without bothering about
a fair trial, if they knew what such a thing was,
they hung the mother while the daughter and
friends could do nothing but look on. Not being
satisfied with the revenge they had taken on her,
they took sharp knives and cut her dead body to

ribbons. It was horrible. All because an Indian mother was forced to kill a white man in defense of a 14-year-old daughter. If the woman had been white and the man an Indian, there probably would have been just as many Indians killed as there were in the tragedy which the Indian boy with the boots cost. The woman would likely have been awarded a medal for her bravery and her name would have gone down in history as one of the bravest of the Pioneers."

Suddenly they heard a loud clatter of hoof beats. Looking out the window to see what was causing so much commotion, the men were surprised to see two women sliding off the back of a panting, lather covered horse. It needed but one glance to show Fred that one of them was Blue Bird. In one jump, he was out the door and running swiftly towards her. He threw his arms around her as she gasped, "Hide me! Hide me! They are after me!"

"They will not get you again!" Fred replied with much determination. He glanced up the river and there he saw a canoe just coming into sight. "They will never get you again," he repeated, "not if I have to get the whole garrison out!"

Sending the two girls into the cabin, he took the horse to a clump of trees and bushes and tied him there out of sight. Bluebird explained in a few words about the scars on her wrists where the cruel rawhide thongs had left their mark and about how she had swum the river to escape her captors.

"And to think," Fred retorted in angry tones, "that only a moment ago, I was raving about the cruelty of the white people. Who are the most heartless people anyway, the Indians or the white people? I am beginning to think that the circumstances will make some people turn into wild beasts no matter what their nationality may be."

Meanwhile, Grey Cloud was storming around on the other side of the river. After all these months of hard work in intensive scheming, his prisoner had escaped. "Of all the ungrateful people," he complained loudly, "she is the worst!"

Well, she could have her white man. She was welcome to him. She would see the day when she would wish that she had listened to her old uncle. But Falling leaf smiled a secret smile as a feeling of thankfulness filled her tired heart. She thought of how the two boys had fooled their father by pretending to be working so hard to get the canoes finished in time to catch their little cousin. All the while they were killing time as much as possible to give her more time to escape. They dared not openly defy their warrior father. Finally, the old man, tired and disgusted, sat down and ran his fingers through his long black hair. He looked at Owl Eyes who sat nearby with a quizzical smile on her face. "Once more," he exclaimed in an angry voice, "the white man wins. Never, never will I trust a white man! I never have and I never will. They say that a dead Indian is a good Indian. Well, I can't say that much for a white man."

CHAPTER XVIII   The Log Cabin

[7]When Fred and Blue Bird had lived in Marcus for about a year, Blue Bird delivered a baby girl. They called her Christine. They had been so very happy together and now the tiny girl was all that was needed to make them so contented that nothing more could be added to their cup of bliss.

Then came their first separation since the time her uncle had kidnapped her. Fred was obliged to go to Portland on business. Blue Bird hated to stay alone. Her old uncle had relaxed his efforts to turn her against her husband, since it did no good. She decided to go visit her mother while she had such a good chance. Grey Cloud had insinuated that her mother would be very happy to see her and the baby. He was careful not to show too much anxiety himself to see his first grandniece of whom he was secretly quite proud.

Although they were all good to her and very attentive to the baby, the months spent there were so long and lonely. They seemed like years. To make it worse, some strange people managed to get into Fred's cabin and steal almost everything Fred had been so long a time accumulating. They even took his home including the land he had homesteaded.

When Fred returned, learning all that had

---

[7] 1870

transpired during his absence, he became discouraged and decided to move to another location. Blue Bird had enjoyed her visit very much, but was happy to get back home.

Fred and Blue Bird took what belongings they still possessed and journeyed to Tshimakian, which in later years became known as Walker's Prairie - named after Elkanah and Mary Walker. The creek which later separated the county and the Spokane Indian Reservation is still called the Tshimakian or in plain English, "Chimokane Creek." At this time, the Tshimakian mission had been discontinued and the Spokane Indians were soon to have another mission built elsewhere on the reservation.

Fred and Blue Bird with their young baby traveled to their new home by way of the Colville Valley, with its rich grassy meadow land dotted with the pretty homes of the settlers. High tree covered mountains stretched along each side of the valley while the lazy little Colville River wended its way happily down the middle. Thick brush grew abundantly along its banks giving shade and shelter to the cattle standing knee deep in the luscious grass, too fat and lazy to move. This was the Valley Beautiful.

When they reached Walker's Prairie, Fred built a log cabin which made them a lovely home. This was the first time since they had lost all they owned at Marcus that they were really happy. The cabin was built on top of a hill so they name the place "Happy Hill."

They were now far enough from all old ties to find
life much more peaceful and a lot safer. This gave
Blue Bird a chance to forget, to a certain extent,
and to forgive the past.

Here Fred settled down to carry on his beloved
work of healing the sick and suffering and, here
once more, he found that this was only one of the
many duties required of him. It did not matter
what other work was given him to do, he was
"Doctor" first and to relieve suffering of mankind
was his main object in life.

As he was not a missionary, he did not do the same
work that the Walkers and Eells did. He did help
the Spokane Indians along in their search for
knowledge. A few of the pupils of the early settlers
had not forgotten the things they had learned. They
were putting their learning to good use by teaching
the other Indians to carry on the good work.
Although Elkanah and Mary Walker were not
allowed to stay there long enough to realize the
great good they had done the Indians, some of the
Indians remembered long after the Walkers were
gone the things they had been taught and became a
good influence to the younger generation. When
another missionary was sent to the Spokanes, he
found able helpers waiting to welcome him.

The experience on this Reservation with smallpox
had caused the tribe to dwindle down until it was
no longer a powerful people. Since the medicine
men had been able to accomplish so little at that

time, Fred had very little difficulty in winning their confidence - in a very short time he had plenty of medical work to keep him busy.

Most of the settlers and all of the Indians were poor so he did not get paid for all he did. He was always satisfied to accept whatever they had to offer in payment. He was contented so long as he was allowed to pursue his own course of happiness, which was to help those who needed his services most. He was not lacking in ambition but was ambitious to succeed in his work only for the love of it and for the sake of humanity. Riches concerned him very little. He had been brought up in wealth and had found no lasting happiness in such a life. Now that he was poor, living in a log cabin with his wife and baby, he was contented, even though there were times when the meals were very plain and their clothes bore many neatly made patches.

One day in the dead of winter, when Christine was about 10 years old, there came a loud knock on the door of the log cabin. She opened the door and there on the doorstep stood an Indian. It was late in the afternoon and the snow was deep. The young man looked as though he had traveled a long way and was cold and hungry. The little girl threw the door open wide as she noticed the worried look on the man's face.

"Come in," she said pleasantly. The man shook the snow off his clothes, drawing his many-colored blanket up closer, walked in and stood beside the fire. He warmed his hands without speaking as his roving eyes wandered around the little cabin.

Just then Fred came in and shook hands with him. "You look tired," he said. "You must have something pretty important to see me about."

"Yes," the Indian replied, "Me come long ways. Our friend Cornelius, very sick. Maybe die. He tell me go get Doctor. Now heap snow, maybe you no can come."

Fred laughed, "No snow can be that deep, not when somebody is that sick, only I'd like to know something about what is wrong with him so I'll know what to take."

"No eat," the man replied, shaking his head. "No eat one week now, no eat, no walk, alla time sleep. Sick - heap sick."

Fred began preparing for his long horseback ride through the deep snow. When duty called, he never questioned his own likes or dislikes. He just obeyed without complaint.

There were two saddle horses in the barn. After the man had been given a warm meal and allowed time to get warm, he was given a fresh horse in place of his own and they started out. They rode all that night and just at break of day, they reached the home of the sick man which was situated on the banks of the Spokane River. In a teepee, lying on some robes and blankets spread out on the ground, was the sick man. Fred knew him quite well as he had often been to Walker's Prairie.

"What's the matter Cornelius? What mischief have you been up to now?" He asked cheerily as he warmed his hands by the blazing fire in the center of the teepee.

"Oh sick, sick!" the old man replied wearily, as he shook his head sadly. "Bimeby die, no can eat. Long time no eat. Medicine Man no good."

Fred laughed as he felt the man's pulse and made him stick out his tongue. Oh, you'll be all right," he said. "You're tough. Never say die. You're going to get well, understand? You'll be well long before spring and be out hunting and fishing again as soon as spring comes."

The old man shook his head weakly, "No," he said. "No get well. Me heap sick, Bimeby die."

From the saddle bag Fred took a package and ordered some hot water. In a few moments, he had some arrow root gruel. He fed it to the man a few drops at a time. He would trust no one with this task for when an Indian became convinced that he was to die, it took all he could do to get back his desire to live. Fred knew that he was the only one in the teepee who believed the man would live. He must work this belief into his patient's mind by giving him the confidence he needed.

The Indian was so weak that he could scarcely raise his head. Fred Hill held him up and fed him very slowly, as he would a baby, until he thought that he had given him all that was good for him. Then he laid the tired man back down on the bed.

"Feel better now?" he asked smiling.

"No. Me heap sick, bimeby die," repeated the old man as he sighed and turned his face to the wall. Fred motioned to the sick man's wife and she followed him out the door.

"Look here," he said earnestly. "Your husband is a very sick man. You must help me. You must tell him that he's going to get well. Don't let him say he's going to die. Just keep telling him that he's going to get well and he'll get well, you'll see.

The woman nodded her head as she gave him a grateful smile. "Me help," she promised, as she wiped away a tear.

Fred stayed with the man for a week. Old Cornelius grew slowly but steadily better. When the weary doctor started for home, the Indian and his family were almost too grateful for words. They knew their loved one would get well just as Fred had told them.

There had been a real Northwestern blizzard during Fred's stay in the Indian camp. The trails were all covered with deep snow. There was not a trace of the old trail leading to Walker's Prairie. Owing to the snow, the landscape was altogether changed so much that Fred had great difficulty finding his way back home.

There were deep snow drifts for his horse to flounder through. The sun was shining brightly but a sharp, cold wind was blowing the snow through the air, striking him in the face and preventing him from getting any warmth from the sunshine. The sun was so bright that he could scarcely see to pick his way. He had never been very familiar with this part of the country. He began to wish he had brought a guide with him. He would have gone back after one but he hated to bother anyone. He felt that as long as he had been in the West, he should be able to find his way around without help.

At times, he would see some familiar sign. He would feel encouraged. Then at other times he felt that he was completely lost. His horse never hesitated to push right along. Suddenly, during one of those times when he had not the faintest idea where he was, he received a frightful shock by finding that he was unable to see. The complete darkness coming up on him so suddenly frightened him. For a moment, he thought it had suddenly grown pitch dark. He pulled his horse to a standstill and tried to figure out what could have happened as he rubbed his eyes in a troubled way. Finally, with a shock, he realized that he was snow blind. "Blind as a bat!" he retorted in great alarm. "Now what will I do? I will freeze to death if I don't get home tonight, but which way is home?" It was here that Fred's many lessons in self-control did him a good turn. When he was almost ready to become panic stricken, he remembered about people who saved their lives by letting their horses find the way home to food and shelter. Acting on this impulse, he tied his reins to the pommel of the saddle and patting his horse on the neck murmured, "Go to it boy. Everything depends on you now."

The faithful animal acted as though he understood for he immediately picked up speed just as though he knew how bad his master needed him. Fred sat thinking as he worked his body to keep up circulation. He knew for the first time just how a blind man must feel with the dog who leads him around. He knew how much the intelligence of his horse meant to him. He had no idea where his horse was taking him. The animal seemed to know and never slackened his pace as he found his way through the deep snow.

Suddenly, the horse seemed to be endowed with new life for Fred knew that he was stepping up faster as if eager to get somewhere fast, as though he knew that his long journey was drawing near the end. The horse nickered and threw his head up just as Fred caught a whiff of something cooking.

A dog barked, then the sweetest music on earth - Christine's voice.

"Oh, Daddy! "she screamed joyfully as he heard her running towards him. Then he felt her hand on his arm. "What's the matter Daddy?" she asked in quick alarm. "You look so strange."

"Just snow blind, dear. Nothing to be alarmed about. Not now, since I'm home at last. I will soon be all right. Just help me off the horse into the house. Have someone attend to the horse. Take good care of him. If it wasn't for him I'm afraid I wouldn't be here."

The girl led her father into the house and piled plenty of wood on the fire. She sent a neighbor boy to care for the horse. She got the weary doctor some hot soup which she fed him herself. She made him as comfortable as possible for it was hard for him to care for himself even at best, owing to the fact that a few years prior to this he had cut his wrist with an ax and as a result had been so unfortunate as to have infection set in which led finally to the amputation of his left arm.

This had not interfered with his work much, as there were always those who were willing to help him whenever he went on calls. His work, being such as it was, he managed to get along fairly well.

It took some time for Fred's eyes to get well but they finally cleared up. The temporary blindness, much to the joy and relief of all, left no bad effects whatsoever.

CHAPTER XIX   Cowboys

[8]Down in California, the Wynecoop family managed to get along fairly well. Curt was always a good industrious boy and never had any trouble getting work. He was good with stock and spent a lot of his time working with stock. When he was not busy with hogs, he was working with cattle on some cattle ranch.

Then, at the time he was in his twenties, he began working at a sawmill. He made good there, but he put most of his wages into lumber and soon had enough with which to build a barn that was needed badly. After that, for a while there was enough to work to keep him and his two brothers busy at home, what with building a new barn and putting other improvements on the place. There was a lot of work to be done and after they had finished the barn they started to work on a rock fence. Part of the fence was built of rocks. Building a rock fence was a long hard job. They split some rails. Rocks were placed on the bottom and the rails to finish off the top. As time and rocks allowed, they built some of the fence of solid rocks and some of all rails. If well built, a good rail fence will last for years. A rock fence is a permanent structure.

The land was good and their crop was grain. They always had a good garden, and as Mandy had seen that a few trees were set out as soon as possible, it was not long until they had plenty of fruit.

---

[8] 1879

Curt was restless at home and could never be satisfied there for long at a time. As soon as he had helped to get their mother settled in her home, he decided that the other two boys could handle the work there and he went to Texas. There, he soon became a full-fledged cowboy, with a job herding cattle and taking them from Texas to Arizona where they were loaded onto the train and shipped back East. This was the sort of work that Curt liked best, for he never tired of handling stock. Best of all, le loved to break colts or horses to ride. He did well at that for there were plenty of horses to break, and not many who knew how to break them. He always tried to break them to be gentle horses. Many others broke them by rough handling and generally succeeded in not only breaking the horses, but in breaking the spirit of the horses, or in making an outlaw of what could have been made into a kind and useful animal. If, by this sort of breaking, the horse did not turn out to be an outlaw, he usually had his spirit broken and soon became too lazy to be a good saddle horse. Like most cowboys in those days, he carried a gun and was an excellent shot. In all his experience as a cowboy, he never had occasion to use his gun on a fellow man. He neither drink, smoked, used tobacco in any form or gambled. He never got into fights as other cowboys did and, in this lack of bad habits, he was unlike most of the cowboys, for he proved that he could be a real cowboy and still be master of himself.

The company he worked with had some trouble

with cattle thieves and on rare occasions one or two men would get caught. Sometimes they would be fortunate enough to capture a whole gang of thieves and such times were usually quite exciting for no gang would give up without a fight. Once the thieves were caught, the cowboys would soon prove what the Wild West was composed of and what it lacked.

Those seeking justice were not necessarily lawless, for the law was considered of very little importance in the West. At such times the thieves were merely taken to a clump of trees and left there. When the cowboys solemnly filed out back to work or to camp they would be minus one rope or two, whatever the case may be, and there would be one or more riderless broncos. Very few words were spoken but every man knew what the rest were thinking about.

Curt never participated in these duties of law enforcement. For one thing, the cattle or horses that the captives had tried to make away with were not any of his, and therefore he did not feel obliged to be present. For another thing, he did not care for that that sort of entertainment, so he usually remained with the cattle.

This is one explanation for the habit the cowboys had of carrying a gun. A cowboy's guns were his law. The other reason was his fear of the Apache Indians, who were always on the watch for a chance to steal anything they could drive, carry away, or to molest the cowboys in many ways.

Curt knew well how to handle his gun and many a rattlesnake lost its head by getting too near him. He always said he hoped the time would never come when he would be compelled to use it on a human being and it never did.

He was riding the range one day. He had lost a favorite horse and was beginning to be quite worried about him. He suspected a certain man by the name of Bill Harem, of knowing something about the horse's whereabouts, and hoped he would meet the man. Suddenly some instinct caused him to glance up quickly and there sat Bill on his horse watching Curt very intently from under his wide-brimmed hat, which he always wore low over his eyes. "Hello Bill," he greeted, very much surprised. "Where are you headed for?"

"Oh, no place in particular," was the answer. "What about you?"

"Out hunting for my bay horse," Curt answered, looking steadily at the man. "Haven't seen him over your way, have you?"

"No I haven't," the fellow replied, almost too quickly Curt noticed, "But say," he continued hastily, "I'll go with you to pass the time away."

Bill was a busy man, so Curt drew his own conclusions. "All right," he agreed cheerfully, "Come along. I never ride alone when I can have company."

The two rode the range together for several hours but found no trace of the stolen horse. Curt allowed Bill to lead the way most of the time and noticed that the man never once ventured anywhere near his own range or the range where his stock would be apt to be grazing at that time. Just to make sure that his suspicions were correct and that he was purposely being steered away from that part of the country, he turned and headed his horse straight towards that direction.

"I don't think you will find him over there!" Bill hastily exclaimed. "I've just been riding that range and saw no horse that looked anything like yours."

This was too much for Curt. He was tired and so was his horse. He knew well enough that Bill was only trying to make a fool of him, and being naturally quick-tempered and impulsive, he resented it.

Immediately whirling on the man, he faced him angrily, his face fiery red, and his blue eyes blazing hotly. "Look here Bill Harem! I believe you stole that horse! I noticed that you were mighty careful to keep me from going near your stock and that can mean only one thing! You've got a pretty good reason for it."

At this Bill swore violently, as he whipped out his revolver. Swift as he was, before he could take aim, he found himself staring down the barrel of a six shooter, inches from his face. Curt was steadily aiming at him and the steely eyes fixed on him spoke volumes. "Throw down the gun!" Curt drawled menacingly.

Bill instantly dropped his gun to the ground.

Lowering his six-shooter, Curt gazed thoughtfully at it for a moment. He had just paid $35 in spot cash that caused him many days of hard work, but it had almost caused him to take a human life. Suddenly he whirled and threw it into the Colorado River. "There!" he exclaimed, a satisfied grin spreading over his face as the gun struck the water about in the middle of the stream. "I'll never aim that gun at another man!"

Bill looked at him in surprise, all fear had disappeared from his eyes, and his face which had been the color of chalk, had begun to resume its natural color. He dismounted from his horse and picked up his gun. Wiping it off carefully, he put it back in the holster. Looking up with perfect understanding in his eyes, he said, "I'll find your horse."

Then he rode away without another word or glance in the direction of the man who had just held his life in his hands and gave it back to him.

The next morning Curt was not a bit surprised to find his bay horse calmly feeding with the rest of his band. "The skunk," he grinned, "I knew as well as anything that he had the horse. Bill turned out 'pretty white' after all. I'll have to give him credit for that."

It had not been so much a sense of fair dealing that
had influenced Bill to a change of heart as the fact
that Curt had known all the while where his horse
was to be found and he was not fool enough to take
too many chances of meeting up with the law
enforcing cowboys, who were the terror of every
horse thief in the country. The mere thought of
them caused Bill to run his hand over his neck. He
realized that he liked neck-tie parties even less
than he liked shooting unarmed men.

After several years of this sort of life, Curt decided
to go back to California. He had no sooner reached
home than his old friends of the plains, Godlik
Garber and Joe Mishler began coaxing him to go
with them to Oregon, or the part of Oregon which
later became the site of Washington. He had
always wanted to go there, so finally decided to
travel along with them, since this promised to be
quite an exploration trip for all of them. The three
boys started for Oregon on horseback. They had a
little money and the best horses they thought could
be found anywhere, but best of all, they were in the
best of health.

They wore chaps made of cowhide, tanned on the
inner side, which left the hair in its natural color.
These were tied onto their legs with strips of
rawhide and they were the best protection a cowboy
could wear against bad weather.

When they reached Mosquito Springs, located near

to what later became Davenport, Washington, the three boys separated. It was there that Curt first met Ed Pelosy, a cattleman.

He was in search of cowboys. He had a large herd of cattle and was short on men, so Curt wasted no time in getting back into his old job of cow punching. They went to Sprague where the cattle were ranging. Here Curt expected to see some sort of a town but all he saw was one half of a built building. Of course, there were not many people but what there were had plenty of horses and that was what he liked. Plenty of horses meant plenty to break and there was nothing he liked better than to break wild horses.

He made a good deal of money at it, too and he was fortunate in seldom getting hurt, and never badly. He never knew when he climbed onto a horse just when or how he would land. Breaking horses was a risky work, and some horses were almost too much for any man.

Curt was exceptionally good at the job and although he was not immune to the act of flying gracefully through the air, he generally lit on his feet and he was never known to let a horse get the best of him. In the end the horse was wise enough to know who was master. It always took a good horse to throw Curt and, strange as it may seem, he always came back for more, until finally the horse, finding that he was not going to win, would become reconciled to the fact and would soon be on the way of becoming a good and useful animal.

One day the people of Walker's Prairie heard of a
man who had red hair reaching over his ears with
long whiskers and a mustache. He was a real
cowboy who never swore, smoke, or drank. This
was hard to believe for never had they heard of
such a cowboy.

As luck would have it, one day the cattle Curt was
tending, wandered away. Curt started out to find
them. He rode for hours, finally coming to some
timber where he thought they might have gotten.

Suddenly he came face-to-face with the prettiest
girl he had ever seen. She was dressed in blue, his
favorite color, and had heavy hair hanging in
braids down her back.

"Whoa there," he shouted, as his horse made a right
about face, and started to run. When he had
quieted the troublesome animal, he turned to look
at the vision, but she had disappeared. "Well if that
don't beat all," he said as he mopped his forehead
with his handkerchief. "I think I must have been
seeing an angel. I'll bet she is the girl I've been
hearing so much about. The one who lives on happy
Hill. Oh, what a happy hill that must be."

A few minutes later he came to a small clearing,
and there before him stood the little log cabin on
Happy Hill. A hitching post stood nearby. To this,
he advanced, dismounted and tied his horse. Then,
with hat pushed back on his head, spurs jingling,
his heart pounding fiercely against his ribs, his

eyes ever alert for a girl in blue, he walked towards the door of the cabin. The door stood open inviting him. As he reached the step, he glanced through the doorway and there in the big chair sat "Doc" Perkins. His hair and long whiskers were as white as snow and he had the look of a man whose days of usefulness were just about over. The quick welcoming expression that instantly overspread his face belied Curt's thoughts immediately. "Come in," came the cordial greeting.

Curt removed his hat and stepped in, hastily glancing around as he accepted the proffered chair.

"I've been looking for some cattle and wondered if you had seen any strays around here?" He said by way of explaining his surprise visit.

"Why, yes," "Doc" as Fred was generally known answered quickly. "I did notice a strange herd of cattle around here just yesterday afternoon. I think they are headed for the hills back there," as he pointed to some hills northeast from the cabin.

Curt was highly pleased. This information relieved the situation a lot he thought. "Thanks," he said. "I suppose this hot weather makes them restless, for I've sure been having a hard time keeping track of them lately. I wonder if I could bother you for a drink. I'm about choked for one, it's so hot.".

At this, Fred quickly rose to his feet, "I'll bet you're about famished for water, this kind of weather," he said remorsefully. "Had any dinner yet? I'll bet you're hungry too."

"No, I haven't," he answered, "but really I'm not a bit hungry." He meant it when he said that, but he still hoped that he would at least get a glimpse of the girl he was getting more anxious to see every moment.

Then he heard a slight sound and glanced hastily towards the doorway leading to the kitchen. His naturally red face turned a bright scarlet, as a blue skirt flipped past the doorway. He resolved to be in no hurry to leave, for he could hear a sweet voice sounding in the other room and he was sure that the owner of the voice would be pretty apt to announce dinner very soon now – "Come to think of it," he thought, "I didn't know I was so hungry."

CHAPTER XX   From Spokane to Happy Hill

About fifty miles from Happy Hill down where the Spokane empties into the Columbia River stood a garrison. It was a beautiful spot on the banks of the Spokane River. The Columbia River could be seen a couple of miles farther down. Trees and hills surrounded the place on all sides.

This was the home to a number of soldiers who were kept there for different purposes according to Army regulation. It was here that Ed Pelosy with Curt Wynecoop and his other cowboys had the job of furnishing the garrison with beef. They found that the quickest and cheapest way to transport the beef was to drive the cattle to the fort, corral and butcher them right there, then sell the meat to a contractor who in turn would sell it to the consumers at the garrison.

Sometimes this was quite a job for some cattle were always trying to break loose and get away. One time a big long-horned steer broke away from them. Some of the boys went after him and in a short time had him cornered. The steer was not to be so easily overcome. Spying one of the cowboys who stood nearby with a vicious looking six gun strapped to his side, the animal lowered his head and, bellowing loudly with tongue hanging out, went after the cowboy.

The cowboy, forgetting all about the faithful gun dangling at his side in his haste to make a getaway, made a wild scramble for the nearest tree and scurried up it like a scared monkey, his shiny spurs jingling, his chaps and six-shooter getting in his way as he finally climbed over the first limb he could reach.

He was just in time as the enraged roar below him testified and in frightened relief the cowboy glanced down to see if he was out of danger, but all he could see was a pair of longhorns making for his beloved wide-brimmed hat, which had cost him a good bit of money and was brand-new. Not even then did he think of the trusty six gun in its holster and in a moment the hat was unrecognizable.

Just then the roar of laughter that reached his ears from the gang of cowboys, who were having so much fun at his expense, was cut short by the loud report of a gun and the roaring, pawing animal fell kicking in the dust.

The crestfallen cowboy slowly slid down from the limb of the tree and picked up his hat with a rueful smile. "Shore fixed my hat," he smiled as he brushed off the dust and put the piece of felt back on his head.

"Yes, he shore did!" one of the boys answered, as he laughed uproariously. "It was worth a dozen hats to see your arms and legs a-grabbing for the tree! Gosh, I'll never forget that for as long as I live."

They never did forget it either. Cowboys have a

habit of remembering such things and springing them on defenseless fellows just at the most embarrassing times. There was no one any better-hearted than a cowboy, but for one of their number to make a fool of himself by climbing a tree to get away from a steer was unforgettable.

If a cowboy got drunk and shot up a town or did some other fool stunt that showed him to be daring and tough, that was to be expected and tolerated. Any cowboy could do anything like that and still hold the respect of his comrades. He must never run from anything, especially when he had a gun strapped to his side. Not if he wanted to stay with the same gang and not unless he was willing to take all the jeering and jousting they cared to hand him.

"Too bad," Curt grinned. By what I've always heard, I supposed that a cowboy might chase a steer up a tree. I never expected to have the fun of seeing it work out the other way around."

The embarrassed cowboy was too busy helping to skin the animal to listen and he did not care to hear any more jokes about cowboys. He was going to quit after supper, anyway.

Curt found many excuses for visiting Happy Hill. The boys soon began to take notice of this and they enjoyed nothing more than to tease him until his face was as red as his fiery hair. It was very seldom that they could make him angry but, if they did, it would end up in nothing more than a lively tussle:

where they rolled on the ground, over and over, sweating and straining until one of them was ready to say he had enough.

Curt was quick and wiry, besides having muscles like iron, and it was seldom that he was the one to give in, so, all the teasing they could do did not prevent him from making his regular trips to Happy Hill, where he always seemed to be a welcome guest.

Curt had been writing to his mother since leaving home and one day he wrote and told her about the wonderful girl he had discovered. He did not try to deceive her in any way. He told her that Christine's mother was an Indian, and wondered at the time what she would think about it.

He remembered so well the terrible fright they had that time out on the plains so many years ago. He knew that his mother had never recovered from it and probably never would. He knew better than anyone else just how much she had always feared Indians since that day and he did not blame her one bit, but he hoped that she would understand about Christine.

When he opened the answer from his letter, he soon saw that he was doomed to disappointment for she had written very severely about her disapproval of his sweetheart.

Curt had not heard from his folks for some time and had been so glad to get the letter he couldn't open it fast enough. For a moment, after he read the contents, he was too stunned to believe his eyes. His pride and independence came to his rescue. "I don't give a rap," he exclaimed angrily as hot, bitter tears stung his eyes. He leaned over and patted his horse with trembling hands as he said shakily, "We don't care, do we, if she is part Indian. She is just as nice and pretty as any white girl and a lot nicer and prettier to my notion! Anyway, I love her like I'm hoping she loves me! I'm going to ask her this very evening to marry me and if she says "Yes" the whole world can go hang for all I care."

After six months, they were married by a man who had ridden many miles on horseback just for that purpose. People from all over the country came to celebrate the occasion. By this time, the country was pretty well settled with white people. They all had a grand time in honor of the best all-around cowboy and the most popular young lady in the country.

Not many years later, about the year 1900, Grey Cloud lived in Marcus. The young folks of the family were living in the log cabin but he much preferred his own comfortable teepee which stood near his very important sweat house. He was feeling rather cross today for the husband of Owl Eyes had only this morning came home drunk and gave her a whipping.

"I know she's mean and maybe deserved the beating, but I hate the fire water that was the cause of all the trouble. That stuff always causes

trouble wherever it is, but when our Indians get it
they go crazy and have no sense at all. I hate those
white people who brought fire water to our people.
Whenever I think of it, I hate everything about
them! Now they are pushing us up into the no-good
rocky parts of our country, or out on the hot and
dry desert places with the jack rabbits and rattle
snakes and expect us to make a living. They call
these places Indian reservations and they really
think we are well treated and should be perfectly
happy at the same time now that they have us
safely out of their way. They settle themselves
comfortably on all our good rich farming land and
wonder why in the world the Indians are always so
poor."

"If we could trust them enough to be sure that, if
we did happen to find something good on our land
and they would not get it away from us, we might
become prosperous and a lot happier. Soon they
will kill all our buffalo and drive all the deer from
the plains. They will spoil our fishing, which is so
important to us, and destroy the land where we
grow our roots and berries. They will get all our
fur-bearing animals and the Indians will have
nothing. We will become weak like children who
have been whipped too much. If some day we
should have war with another country, our children
will fight side by side with our white neighbors."

"I'm getting too old now so all day I sit and think.
No more do I ride my ponies over my wide prairies.
No more do I own any prairies, and I'm lucky to
have one or two ponies to ride to the huckleberry

mountains once a year or to the store. We are poor and we will always be poor. When many of the white people are rich or when we have made them rich, we will still be poor."

I never trusted the white people. When I was young and foolish, I told them so with my bow and arrows and sometimes with my tomahawk, but they came like grasshoppers! It was no use - White men! Bah! White men! Fire water!! White men!! Cheat!! Alla time cheat!! I don't like to think of them. It makes me sick because I get so mad."

"Maybe, bimeby, I go happy hunting grounds. Then white men say, Great Cloud good Injin now! Ugh! Ugh!!"

Shaking his long grey hair from his eyes, the old man reached for his cane and made his way to his sweat house. Here, still grumbling to himself, he built a fire and heated some rocks which were piled in the middle of the sweat house. The sweat house was only two or three feet high in the middle and was about six feet wide at the bottom. It looked like a huge mushroom, except that it was fastened to the ground all around with a small hole in one side for a door. Grey Cloud removed all his clothing and left them outside the door. Then being careful that the sweat house was tightly closed, he took some water and sprinkled it on the hot rocks which instantly filled the sweat house with not steam.

After that, Grey Cloud was too busy to think of anything else. He was very happy as he vigorously scrubbed himself thoroughly while the hot steam loosened every particle of dirt and opened up the pores of his skin. When this was done, he opened the sweat house door and slowly crawled out on his hands and knees. Within a few feet of the sweat house, a cold mountain stream was running merrily over the rocky creek bottom. To this Grey Cloud made his way as he leaned heavily on his cane and, walking out into the cold stream, began throwing the cold water all over his perspiring body.

After a few moments of this, he went back to the sweat house. He felt better now, much better. He then decided to take a nap, so getting back into his clothes, which was another reason why he hated civilization, he laid down in the warm sunshine and went to sleep.

There we leave Grey Cloud, his resentful heart at last finding contentment in blessed sleep, a balm for weary hearts of people of every nation.

Not many years later, Doctor Perkins reached the end of the trail, a trail not so long in years but every year crammed full. It was just a year or two after Blue Bird had bade him farewell to wait on the other shore. The name of F.W. Perkins was almost forgotten by all except those who knew him best, and by those who loved him most.

In spite of all his years of usefulness, he died a man poor in this world's goods. He died as he lived, thinking of others. He had lived unselfishly and he died the same way, just as his grandfather had done so many years ago, and just as his father and uncle had done, busy up to the last moment.

The End

- Millie LeBret (Joe's mom) twin brother found this fawn orphaned on Spokane Reservation brought it home and their cow raised it.

- Mom (Millie LeBret) with her horse socks in front of her house in Wellpinit.

- Herb Lyons (Joe's dad) setting choker, Merrit Galbraith on the cat, Spokane Reservation (1942?)

- Joe's mom (Millie LeBret) and Joe's dad (Herb Lyons) wedding in Presbyterian Church in Wellpinit 1939.

- Loaded up to move in 1944 to (west) of the hills above Wild Rose Prairie Mom (Millie), Dad Herbert, and Joe in the middle in front of Mom's house in Wellpinit. *on the wagon*

- Mom standing by Wagon, ready to leave Wellpinit to move. Notice nursing *colt.*

• My Dad Herbert Lyons and Joe moving dirt in a slip scraper at the house we moved to above (west) of Wild Rose Prairie.

James Le Bret & Frances' (Wynecoop) store on left and house in Wellpinit, Spokane Tribe Reservation, Washington State.

Editor's Notes

When Ben Cabildo of CMTV told me about Joe Lyons and his grandmother Frances's journal I was excited to meet with him and the results greatly exceeded my expectations. The journal entitled Echo of the Tom Toms by Frances Le Bret is a great account of a historical story that needs to be told of the daily lives of the pioneers and Indians of the Spokane and Colville area, a story the history books didn't teach in school.

While editing the grammar and punctuation, I was careful to leave the story in the words and language of the writer. After a discussion with Joe Lyons the owner of the journal and Frances' grandson as to whether words that are now considered offensive should be included, it was decided that the story should be told in the words used in the 1940's by the author, Frances Le Bret. The editors apologize in advance for any offense taken.

Thanks to :
Gary A. Edwards, Editor.
www.EdwardsMusicSite.com
Joe Lyons, Editor and Copyright Owner.
Warren Seyler – DNR, Provided over 500 Spokane Tribe Historical photos
Roger Cochran for his support for this project.
Larry Telles and members of the IWL in North Idaho for suggestions about fonts used in the 19th century.
Special thanks to CMTV Spokane Washington who plan to broadcast this story on Channel 14 Comcast

Cable. For more information Contact CMTV at
http://community-minded.org

Echo of the Tom Toms by Frances Le Bret,
Copyright © 2017 by Joe Lyons. All rights reserved.
Available on Amazon.com.

Made in the USA
Lexington, KY
15 August 2017